The Immorality of Limiting Growth

The Immorality of Limiting Growth.

Edward Walter

State University of New York Press   ALBANY

Published by
State University of New York Press, Albany

© 1981 State University of New York

For information, address State University of New York
Press, State University Plaza, Albany, N.Y., 12246

Library of Congress Catlaoging in Publication Data
Walter, Edward, 1932-
  The immorality of limiting growth.
  Bibliography: p.
  Includes index.
  1. Economic development. 2. Liberalism. I. Title.
II. Title: Limiting growth.
HD88.W34   338.9   81.166
ISBN 0-87395-478-5   AACR2
ISBN 0-87395-479-3 (pbk.)

Contents

Introduction

The overriding motivations for writing this book were, first, to rebut the arguments of what I call "no-growth futurists," who contend that the industrial stage of history is over and must be replaced by a steady-state society and, second, to defend the liberal theory of government.

When I first read *The Limits of Growth,* by Donella and Dennis Meadows and their colleagues, one of the best known books in the no-growth library, I was impressed by the evidence which seemed to show that the world could no longer rely on industrial growth to provide social prosperity because of the exponential growth of pollution and population and the exponential depletion of natural resources and agricultural land that accompany industrial growth. At the same time, I reacted against the proposed solutions. The Meadows suggested that the world could be saved from social collapse only by the institution of a steady-state society. In such a society, industrialization would be slowed down until growth were slight, pollution and population growth were reduced, and agricultural production were increased. Wealth would be redistributed to the advantage of the developing nations and to the disadvantage of the countries of the first world (the United States, Great Britain, France, West Germany, Japan, and so on). I rejected these recommendations because I believed them to be unrealistic, the "ivory tower" proposals of academics. I wondered how it would be possible to convince first-world nations to give up some of their wealth so that developing nations could improve their economies. I asked, How can multi-national corporations be convinced to restrict their growth so that natural resources would be available for future generations? My first impression was that these things had to be done on moral grounds, but I was convinced that they would never be successfully undertaken because entrenched economic, social, and political factions are resolutely selfish and congenitally shortsighted. In holding this view, I am both an unregenerate Hobbesian (Hobbes claimed that people are fundamentally selfish) and a skeptic who believes that political and social institutions are morally corrupt. I base this latter belief on my observations of the brutal treatment of labor by capitalists, the duplicity of social and political institutions in handling racial minorities, and the mendacity of governments in conducting international relations and pursuing war.

Besides suspecting that the recommendations of no-growth futurists were unrealistic, I objected to the fact that they placed the burden of reconstruction on the first world. I opposed this for two reasons. First, strains on the economies of these countries would hurt the indigenous poor more than any other group. Entrenched social classes would use their political power to protect themselves from economic deprivation. In the United States, racial minorities, independent farmers, migrant workers, and unskilled laborers would suffer immeasurably. Second, the industrial way of life is socially desirable because it has brought about improved medication, sanitation, nutrition, living conditions, and, in my opinion, can continue to do so. I view industrialization as the practical expression of the scientific temperament and technological innovation as the means of improving social life. Technology and science have increased life expectancy and lowered the death rate. That people live longer is a major reason for overpopulation, the intensification of pollution, and the scarcity of land. I opposed solving contemporary problems by giving up the advantages provided by technology and science. No-growth futurists blithely ignore the positive legacy of industrial society. It is an easy situation to parody. These people work in offices that are air-conditioned in summer and centrally heated in winter. They collect data from sophisticated computers and record their findings on electric typewriters. Moreover, they travel around the country in jet airliners, preaching that people should abandon technology and science and return to nature.

The situation as I saw it was that an energy-environmental crisis was imminent; nations would not adopt remedial measures because of chronic myopia and selfishness; and the people who were aware of the dangers (no-growth futurists) were proposing "ivory tower" solutions.

I began research with two goals in mind. Primarily, I wanted to find realistic solutions that would not place the burden of redress on any group. In other words, I was looking for policies that would neither require an improvement in human nature nor force any region, nation, or social group to sacrifice its well-being for the improvement of others. I wanted policies that would distribute burdens equitably. I also hoped that the liberal form of government would remain a viable medium of change. My desire was not based on sentimentality or parochialism. I believed (and continue to believe) that the greatest threat to humankind comes from the tendency of people to act tyrannically, a tendency that the liberal form of government is designed to control. For this reason, I hoped that it need not be abandoned. Secondarily, I wanted to check the validity of the claims made by no-growth futurists. I knew that experts in the area disagreed with the group's findings, but I was not sure of the extent or nature of the disagreement.

I therefore entered into a long, intensive period of research. Not being a scientist, I was forced to acquire familiarity and facility with new technical languages, principles, and research techniques. I found this study fascinating and immeasurably rewarding, but I have not become an expert in either the natural or social sciences. I remain a philosopher—specifically a political and moral philosopher. Although I think that I have acquired enough skill to evaluate the resource-environmental crisis, I cannot offer my own technological theories for averting the danger. I can only rely on the data and theories of experts. I hope, however, that I can address the moral questions with more completeness and insight than most natural and social scientists can. And, I think that I am aware of the political ramifications of remedial action unlike many scientists.

My conviction is that the world is not running out of most resources. I believe that the energy crises of 1973 and 1979 were primarily caused by political maneuvering and poor planning. However, I am convinced that there are real shortages of certain resources. These shortages can be overcome, I believe, by intensifying technological research. Not only do I consider the claim of no-growth futurists that the industrial stage of history is over to be incorrect, but I contend that the solution to the resource-environmental crisis is, in fact, a new burst of technological innovation.

On the other hand, there are certain claims of no-growth futurists with which I agree. Pollution, overpopulation, and the nuclear arms race present awesome threats to human existence. All have to be controlled if we are to preserve civilized life on this planet.

If my commitment to the liberal theory of government did not waver initially, when it appeared to me that the claims of no-growth futurists were true, it was strenghtened when I concluded that many of the most important of these claims were actually false. In this book, I will argue that liberal democracy remains a viable form of government, that the moral goals on which this system is based are attainable despite the present resource-environmental crisis, and that the technological and material growth to which liberal democracy is committed are still justifiable means of furthering human development. In short, a liberal program for the future is tenable.

Liberalism, being a moral and political theory as well as an active political movement, can be easily misunderstood and misinterpreted. Confusion between theory and practice arises because some liberals seek a particular liberal goal (for example, greater economic opportunities and social rights for racial minorities) without being aware of its philosophical basis. Consequently, they may adopt nonliberal means of obtaining the desired end. Others may be enamored of certain aspects of liberal theory but may ignore the social changes that have made some traditional liberal practices obsolete. These people may talk in the 1980s like the English Whigs of 1797.

In order to provide a coherent definition of liberalism and to demonstrate its adequacy for serving contemporary needs, I will develop an *essential liberalism.* In so doing, I will attempt to mediate between classical liberalism (the theory of the English Parliamentarians of the seventeenth century, John Locke, and Adam Smith) and contemporary liberalism (the theory of John Dewey, John Kenneth Galbraith, Harry Girvetz, and Robert Dahl). I will try to show that certain principles have been upheld throughout the history of liberalism and are useful in the current situation. I hope to demonstrate that there are unalterable liberal *ends* and *means* but that liberalism is flexible enough to respond to social and environmental change. Specifically, I will maintain that liberalism is an adequate mechanism by which society can overcome the present resource-environmental crisis.

By contending that liberalism is a viable moral and political philosophy, I risk being dismissed as a "twentieth-century dinosaur" because many moral and political thinkers consider liberalism a failed philosophy. However, I believe that disenchantment with liberalism is based on the fact that liberalism cannot produce a utopia. My fear is that many antiliberal theorists will cast off the good in pursuit of an unrealizable ideal. I will argue that alternative political systems theorized by critics of liberalism cannot achieve desirable goals without creating the political tyranny that liberal government is meant to avoid. Would it be an achievement to supply humankind with food, resources, and protection from environmental hazards at the cost of human freedom? I think not. I believe that human freedom is compatible with social and economic security.

During this study committed to liberal philosophy, I have guarded against the temptation to interpret the evidence in such a way that the principles of liberalism are unfailingly upheld. I have applied the lesson I learned from the philosopher Karl Popper. He maintained that every theorist must employ a "principle of falsifiability;" that is, every theorist is required to identify clearly and unequivocally the conditions under which his theory might be shown to be untrue. If any of these conditions exist, then the theory is untenable. If a principle of falsifiability is not used, then the argument may beg the question. Therefore, I have included such a principle in my development of an essential liberalism.

1. The Challenge to Industrial Society: No-Growth Futurism

A new form of pessimism, called "no-growth futurism," has come into vogue. Its proponents claim that Western society is headed for collapse because the people of the West have blind faith in the capacity of technology to solve society's problems, even though the industrial age is over. Traditionally, in the West, recovery from social calamity has been achieved by a burst of industrial growth through technological innovation. Westerners do not realize, according to no-growth futurists, that the industrial age is merely a stage in history and that historical stages last for only a finite period.

No-growth futurists claim that industrial society is obsolete because we are reaching a point of confrontation with the *finiteness* of the *earth's* arable land and resources. Furthermore, we are approaching this point at an exponential rate.

In the future, international tensions will increase because of the unequal distribution of the world's wealth. Furthermore, the causes of social collapse will be so deeply rooted as to be irreversible. The distribution of food, medical services, and material goods will be disorganized, which will cause the death rate to accelerate. Governments will be rent with dissension because the rich will seek to retain their wealth, while the growing numbers of poor will seek to increase their share of dwindling food supplies and goods. The conditions will resemble those of Medieval Europe when the Black Death ravaged the countryside. All of these dire consequences will take place if hostilities between "have" and "have not" nations do not intensify to such an extent that a world war ensues. The probability of war will increase at an accelerating rate as economic conditions worsen. Finally, in the unlikely event that factors mitigating the aforementioned conditions intervene, the natural environment will be rendered uninhabitable by pollution.

All of this will come to pass, it is maintained, if business proceeds as usual. Standing in the way of social and ecological restoration, and the psychological cause of the problem, is *blind faith in industrial growth through technological innovation*. This faith persists because technological innovation has been the unfailing means by which society has recovered from economic depression since the Industrial Revolution began two centuries ago. Doomsday predictions have been made before—most recently, during the Great Depression of the 1930s—but doomsday has not come. Nevertheless, no-growth futurists insist that it is no longer possible to escape destruction by traditional means. They believe that there must be a change in the attitude of the public. People must be convinced that social salvation requires the development of a steady-state society, that is, a society in which industrial growth, pollution, and population growth are stabilized and food production and land cultivation are maximized. No-growth futurists intend to promote this change in attitude by purposely devaluing material consumption and extolling the virtues of living in natural surroundings unspoiled by industry and the automobile and of family planning. The long-term consequences will be a decrease in industrial production, the preservation of natural resources, the restoration of a clean environment, and a reduction in population.

Another dire prediction made by no-growth futurists is that the gap between rich and poor nations will grow exponentially. To solve this problem the industrial West will have to share its technological expertise and agricultural wealth with the developing nations of the world.

No-Growth Futurists

The term "no-growth futurist" refers to a group of social scientists who engage in predicting world trends, specifically in relation to the economic, ecological, demographic, and political conditions that collectively comprise social living. These social scientists have consciously resurrected the Malthusian theory of population. Malthus argued that, since populations grow exponentially whereas agricultural productivity increases only arithmetically, a struggle for existence arises in which populations are stabilized by the natural processes of disease, famine, and war. Malthus claimed that, by providing food, shelter, and medical care for the poor, social reformers would disrupt the balance of nature. Eventually a devastating depression would occur because there would not be enough food for everyone. In essence, nature, by selecting the strong as survivors, benefited humankind, whereas the well-intentioned actions of social reformers would create disaster by upsetting the natural order.

Malthus's thesis was eventually rejected when advances in agriculture and industrial technology made social reform with its attending population booms compatible with economic prosperity. No-growth futurists

have revived the Malthusian theory, expanded its application to resource depletion, pollution intensification, land despoilment, and inflation. Moreover, the theory has been given new credibility by the use of
computers. With this method of calculation, social prognostications are
now considered to be on the level of science.

Although no-growth futurists retain the original Malthusian point—
that populations grow faster than the supply of food—they decidedly
reject the Malthusian belief that famine, disease, and war should be
allowed to reestablish the balance of nature. They are social reformers
and use Malthus' thesis to justify goals that he would have found repug-
nant and iniquitous. By and large, they share contemporary liberal
goals: to reduce chances of war (especially nuclear war), to control the
polluting practices of industry, and to redistribute the world's wealth to
the benefit of developing nations. Malthus believed it was good that
nature favored the strong; no-growth futurists treat Malthus' strong as
if they are evil.

The principal no-growth futurists are those who conducted research
on behalf of the Club of Rome, an informal group of industrialists and
intellectuals who were disturbed by world trends and sought confirma-
tion of their fears by professional and academic scholars. Those who
conducted the initial research were Donella and Dennis Meadows, Jay
Forrester, and Mihajlo Mesarovich and Eduard Pestel.[1] Of these original
writings, the Meadows' popular book, *The Limits of Growth*, came as a
bombshell. It made the public conscious of growth problems as it had
not been before. Actually, dire predictions for similar reasons had been
made by social scientists, economists, and environmentalists for several
decades before the Club of Rome came into existence. Such people as
Daniel Bell, E. J. Mishan, and Barry Commoner were highly critical of
the growth policies of industrial society. There are differences, however,
in the reasoning of the Club of Rome scholars and the latter futurists.
For example, Barry Commoner does not claim that we are running out
of natural resources. Rather, the impending disaster will be precipitated
by the single-minded efforts of industry to make profits. As a consequence, Commoner concludes that current industrial practices are irrational and destructive. Salvation cannot be achieved through the establishment of a no-growth economy, but by rational planning.

As the thesis of this book is developed, the reader will see that Commoner's desire for rational economic planning is quite reasonable.
Actually, I do not place all of those who claim that social disaster is
imminent in the same category. Nevertheless, I will use the evidence
gathered by Commoner, Mishan, and others to support no-growth

claims in order to present the no-growth theory as powerfully as possible. In summary, two groups will be considered: (1) those who contend that social disaster is possible because of poor industrial, environmental, economic, and/or social planning (Commoner et al.) and (2) no-growth futurists who state that the industrial age is over and fundamentally oppose industrial growth. In this book, the expression "no-growth futurist" will refer exclusively to those who believe that society can be saved from disaster *only* by instituting a steady-state society.

Despite the differences between these two groups, a common no-growth consciousness has developed. The publicity given to *The Limits of Growth* has created a bandwagon effect. Many liberals who were only dimly aware of the subtleties of the new application of Malthusian theory, joined the no-growth chorus because no-growth futurism is hard on big business, a frequent target of contemporary liberals. Many environmentalists and ecologists, fearing that fragile ecosystems would be endangered by industrial expansion and pollution, also joined the crusade.

How these divergent forces formed a common faction is exemplified by the oil crisis of 1973. To no-growth futurists the crisis verified their claim that resource depletion requires a shift to a steady-state society. Liberals condemned industry for precipitating the crisis for venal purposes. Environmentalists singled out the oil industry as a prime cause of ecological degradation. All of these groups, for different reasons, supported federal legislation aimed at slowing energy growth by increasing the cost of energy consumption.[2] A similar consensus evolved during the oil crisis of 1979.

Before the claims of the no-growth futurists are discussed, it should be made clear that there are two targets: specifically, the Club of Rome researchers and, generally, those who claim that the industrial age is over. The major emphasis here will be on the contentions of the former group because their work has received great attention.

In the subsequent sections of this chapter, the no-growth thesis will be elaborated. So that it is given a fair hearing, it will be supported by as much evidence as possible. As explained above, this will entail citing the work of others who are not no-growth futurists but who agree with particular no-growth findings.

The Guiding Principles of No-Growth Futurism

No-growth futurists contend that three general facts about social systems are generally ignored. (1) Social systems are organic wholes in which each structure or institution causally influences all other social structures or institutions. (2) The actions of most social structures or institutions lead to *exponentially* manifested social consequences. (3) There is a time gap of considerable duration between the performance of a social action and its consequences.

The relationship between resource depletion and agricultural growth exemplifies the claim that social structures are organic wholes. Currently, there is a desire to produce more food. The use of sophisticated technology can satisfy this desire. As the manufacture of farm machinery increases to meet the need of expanding agricultural production, more factories will have to be constructed and more machines to manufacture farm machinery will have to be built. All of this activity will deplete the supply of natural resources. When people think superficially about the use of natural resources, they imagine that resources are employed only to manufacture consumer goods. But, in fact, they are used in *every* phase of manufacture. No-growth futurists emphasize the great strain that is brought to bear on the natural resource system because a relative increase in agricultural production produces a relative decrease in the supply of natural resources. No-growth futurists contend that representatives of each institution (agriculturists in our example; industrialists or economists in other contexts) *act* as if their institution had no influence on other institutions.

The second claim, that the consequences of social actions manifest exponentially, is an updated version of Malthus' tenet that population grows geometrically. The standard example of exponential growth concerns a king who is asked to give someone a single gold piece on one day, to double that amount on the next day, and to double the amount of the previous day on each subsequent day. As every grade-school child knows, the king's fortune will be depleted in a very short time. No-growth futurists apply this notion of growth in a variety of contexts.

The third point, that there is a time lag between an action and its consequences, can be made clear by a simple analogy. When a cancer first develops in a person, there is little generalized influence on the person's health. In fact, the cancer is rarely detected in the initial phase because few effects are observable. When the symptoms are manifested to the host, it is generally too late to cure the disease. Silently and painlessly, the cancer has progressed, has spread to so many organs that the removal of the cancerous cells result in the destruction of essential organs. If the cancer had been detected earlier a simple surgical procedure might have restored the patient's health. The presence of toxic materials in cigarettes does not affect the smoker immediately. But over a twenty-year period of intense smoking, cigarettes are capable of producing cancer, heart disease, emphysema, and so on. When the smoker becomes aware of the symptoms of the disease that afflict him, it is usually past the time when remedial work can cure him.

No-growth futurists have the conviction that social scientists habitually distort reality by treating each subject as if it were essentially independent of every other subject. The economist separates his subject from psychology and political science; the sociologist ignores the insights of the psychologist; and the philosopher remains a recluse in his ivory tower, where he is content to stay.

The approach of no-growth futurists can be characterized as *organic*. Thus far, the organic view has been applied to the relationship between social institutions and natural conditions, for example, the relationship between agricultural growth and natural resource depletion or between farming and economics. No-growth futurists apply the organic view to international relations as well. They charge that nations and geographical regions are viewed by politicians, social scientists, and ordinary citizens as separate entities. However, nations and geographic regions are integrated systems; they are, in fact, "one world." Enormous improvements in transportation, communication, and technology, which have enabled manufacturing companies of one nation to interact with raw material suppliers of other nations, have produced this new reality.

Finally, no-growth futurists contend that people assume incorrectly that the earth's resources are infinitely bountiful, that oil or tin or arable land will always exist in sufficient amounts to satisfy human desires and needs. No-growth futurists argue that every resource is limited—space and air, as well as oil, tin, and arable land.

The Specific Claims of No-Growth Futurists

No-growth futurists apply these guiding principles to industrialization, resource depletion, pollution, agricultural production, and world population.[3] Their findings, then, are applied to economic systems.

Industrialization

The tendency of industry is to grow, that is, to produce more material goods. Traditional explanations for this process of continuous growth is that material goods are necessary for a satisfying life and that industrial growth is the means, and the *only* means, by which material goods are effectively distributed among people. No-growth futurists contend that the consequences of industrial growth are far-reaching, unexpected, and deleterious. They are as follows:[4]

1. The environment is degraded by industrial waste, which has the side effect of creating health hazards, decreasing the availability of land, and bringing about a deterioration of the water supply.

2. Natural resources are depleted, which causes prices to rise in order to meet the cost of exploring for remote resources.

3. Pollution increases as "unclean" resources (such as shale oil and coal) are substituted for the depleted resources.

4. Land used for industrial expansion becomes unavailable for agriculture and housing, both of which are, and will continue to be, in short supply.

5. The ecological conditions necessary for human habitation are altered by increased industrial expansion and urbanization.

6. The appreciable gap between rich and poor nations will widen because technology and wealth are centered in particular regions of the world.

Initially, it is said, the advantages of industrialization will remain in the developed nations. This will intensify the starvation of the undeveloped and developing nations.[5] Eventually, however, economic and political power will shift from the developed nations to the developing nations because the developing nations possess most of the natural resources and can produce goods at lower prices.[6]

Technological innovation will be too expensive to save the world from disaster. The cost of research will increase because natural resources are expended in the very practice of experimentation. This means that investment costs will become so prohibitive that profits will be insufficient to justify investment. Moreover, some innovative industrial techniques, such as the use of nuclear power, have devastating ecological side effects. Waste produced by a nuclear power plant is equivalent in radioactive power to about 2,500 tons of radium. If these wastes were released into the environment, they would kill 100 times more people than reside in a city of average size. Furthermore, nuclear wastes persist and have to be isolated in storage facilities for approximately 200,000 years.[7] No-growth futurists doubt that industry can be trusted to safeguard against nuclear accidents. They cite the frequency of oil spills in recent years. They observe how forests have been stripped by lumber manufacturers and how land has been despoiled by mining companies. No-growth futurists blame these destructive practices on industrial management's single-minded pursuit of profit. Management simply ignores the effects of its products on the consumer and the environment.

No-growth futurists deny that government can effectively regulate industrial nuclear use. They argue that industry can bring such weight to bear on a legislature that official policy will tolerate industrial abuses.

They note, for example, that the U.S. government has not been able to force the automotive industry to manufacture nonpolluting cars despite the fact that the technology has been available for some time. Detroit automobile manufacturers seek and obtain delays in altering their products because design changes would eat into their profits. And while the U.S. government pours millions of dollars into a campaign to convince people to stop smoking cigarettes, it supplies many more millions of dollars to the cigarette industry to stimulate production. Even though this double standard has been made public and soundly criticized by the press, the legislature is too much a servant of industry to adopt a consistent policy.

No-growth futurists add that, even if a successful means of avoiding nuclear accidents were found, the use of nuclear power would still be undesirable because too much land needed for agriculture and housing would have to be used for the storage of nuclear wastes. As the reliance on nuclear power grew, more and more land would have to be so used.

Depletion of Natural Resources

The heart and soul of industrial society is the utilization of natural resources. Energy provided by oil, natural gas, and coal runs factories, heats and cools homes, and powers automobiles and airplanes. Metals are used to manufacture products, to make machines which produce goods, and to construct buildings. As previously noted, society treats these resources as though they were inexhaustible. No-growth futurists point out that most natural resources are nonrenewable; that is, once they are used, they cannot be replaced naturally. In cases in which a resource can be replaced, the process is too slow for practical use in the foreseeable future.[8]

No-growth futurists claim that most current industrial estimates of future resource availability are inaccurate because they are based on the assumption that resources are consumed at a constant rate.[9] However, the growth of industry to meet the needs of an expanding population and to satisfy the desire of a consumer society for material goods leads to a rapid decrease in the supply of nonrenewable resources. As shortages become acute, all of the processes noted previously, such as the escalation of investment costs relative to profits, will occur.

It is argued that society ignores the problem and refuses to conserve natural resources. For example, even though energy prices rose after the oil crisis of 1973, Americans continued to use automobiles as much as ever. For a time, the sale of motor trailers declined and summer resorts had fewer patrons. After two seasons, however, these trends were reversed. Even though studies show that setting the speed limit at 55 miles per hour reduces gas consumption, most Americans would like the speed limit to be increased.[10] We can expect similar reactions once the current oil crisis is over.

It is said that people will not change their attitudes and habits because they believe that innovative techniques—actually, technological miracles—will rescue society from social and ecological disaster at the eleventh hour.[11] The response of no-growth futurists to these expressions of faith is that, even if technological breakthroughs could save industrial society, the failure to plan for them *now* is dangerous. If nothing is done, the gap between the goods available and the needs of a materialistic society will be so great when shortages become apparent that an enormous effort and immeasurable time will be needed to bring about a technological miracle. Consequently, by the time a technological miracle occurs, social unrest will already have assumed gigantic proportions.

Pollution

Just as natural resource depletion and industrialization grow exponentially, pollution of the natural environment continues at an exponential rate, according to no-growth futurists. Like natural resource depletion and industrial growth, pollution has a disastrous effect on human welfare. No-growth futurists consider the natural environment to be an integrated whole composed of a variety of systems in which the destruction of a part endangers the existence of other parts. Indirectly, then, human life is threatened because of the misuse of the atmosphere, water, soil, and other living things. The cause of the gradual deterioration of the environment is exponential industrial growth and population growth.

In passing, it should be mentioned that many of these claims are shared by environmentalists. However, many environmentalists believe that industrialization can be harmonized with ecological well-being if rigid pollution safeguards are introduced. Furthermore, some environmentalists ignore the population problem. Even though no-growth futurists desire pollution controls, they tie environmental salvation to other remedies. A cure can be effected, no-growth futurists claim, by stabilizing population and industrialization, as well as reducing pollution.

Let us look at the specific claims of no-growth futurists. When chemicals are released into the air by industrial processes, human beings breathe in poisons that might cause disease. The best known example of air pollution is the case of Los Angeles smog. In July 1943, residents of Los Angeles were shocked to see the air turn to a whitish haze.[12] This condition persisted and produced eye and throat irritation in many people. Eventually the smog dissipated but returned for increasingly long periods of time. Smog is produced by the action of sunlight on pollutants in the air.[13] Originally, the release of hydrocarbons by the burgeoning petroleum industry caused the deterioration of the air. Later, as this problem was met by rigid controls, emissions from automobiles produced smog.[14]

At this late date, it is claimed that the poisoning of air by automobile emissions has not been eliminated. Nor is smog unique to Los Angeles. For some time, means have been available to redesign the automobile engine so that the release of the deadly substance nitrogen dioxide into the air is reduced. However, the automotive industry has used its political influence to hold back federal legislation that would require strict controls.

No-growth futurists note that air in industrialized cities contains more than photochemical smog. A 1963 study demonstrated that the air in a number of cities in the United States contains chemical substances not found in "natural" air.[15] Most of these substances are by-products of industrial activity. Laboratory experiments suggest that they create health hazards. It is feared that, since these chemicals are present in small amounts and are breathed in for years, their effect could be irreversible.

The atmosphere provides a shield that protects the earth from excessive heat and radiation. The energy consumption of industrial society leads to the release of an increasing amount of heat into the air, which may significantly raise the earth's temperature. It has already been observed that urban centers have become "thermal islands." The long-range consequences of such environmental conditions are, at the present time, merely a matter of scientific speculation.[16]

One possible consequence is that the next ice age will be held off for some time—possibly two hundred years.[17] Whether the result will be felicitous is questionable. Uncertainties abound when changes in the atmosphere are artificially induced. Will killer storms occur more frequently? Will tidal waves be more destructive? Will atmospheric changes produce more deserts and wastelands? No-growth futurists warn that conditions may be deadly and that there will be insufficient time to reverse them. The question they ask is: Do we want to gamble the future away simply because we do not want to control our consumption of resources?

The upper stratosphere contains ozone, which protects living beings from ultraviolet radiation. Ozone is a molecule composed of three atoms of oxygen. In the early years of the earth, before oxygen and ozone were formed, ultraviolet radiation was so intense that living things remained under the protective cover of water. Only after an ozone layer was formed could animals move to dry land and biological and social evolution take place. It is reasonably certain, say no-growth futurists (and environmentalists), that a depletion of ozone would have serious consequences for the sustenance of life. At the very least, there would be a significant rise in the incidence of human cancer. At the worst, it would be impossible for human life to continue. Nonetheless, industry continues to produce and use aerosol cans even though scientific studies show that their use depletes the supply of ozone in the atmosphere.

Pollution endangers important water systems. The no-growth futurist can cite the case of Lake Erie to exemplify the danger we are facing. This 12,000-year-old lake at one time teemed with life. Sturgeon, northern pike, cisco, and whitefish abounded. Now, although the total fish catch remains approximately the same, these valuable fish have all but disappeared and have been replaced by "rough" fish—perch, carp, sheephead, and catfish.[18] An insufficient amount of oxygen in the water is directly responsible for this change. During the hot summer months, fish descend to the lake bottom where the temperatures are cooler. However, when oxygen is in short supply, the more active fish (the sturgeon, cisco, and so on) cannot survive, whereas the less active scavenger fish can.[19] Waste products do not flow from the lake into the sea because they are trapped by previously deposited waste products that have sunk to the lake bottom. Then, the waste products are eventually reconverted to huge algal blooms, which use up the oxygen essential for sustaining noble fish. It is maintained that the problem was caused by the use of Lake Erie as a dumping ground for industrial and municipal organic wastes and for agricultural fertilizer drainage.[20]

What happened to Lake Erie is not unusual, only dramatic. No-growth futurists contend that such abuse of the environment is typical in the industrial world. They argue that another result of depositing organic and inorganic matter into bodies of water is the creation of new and dangerous diseases by soil organisms growing in the polluted water. It has been shown that the bacterial count of polluted waters rises.[21] For example, swimmers at European beaches are twice as likely to acquire infections as nonswimmers.[22] These waters show the higher bacterial counts associated with increases in organic pollution from sewage and industrial wastes.

In summary, pollution is said to threaten the ecological balance that is necessary to sustain life. Thermal heating, the destruction of waterways, and alterations in the atmosphere may make this planet uninhabitable for human beings. Furthermore, pollution directly affects human health. The degradation of the environment is accelerating as industrial growth continues and as population grows.

The discovery of the pesticide DDT in fish is cited by the no-growth futurist. It is predicted that many years will pass before DDT is no longer found in living things.[23] No-growth futurists note the increasing amount of mercury being released into water. The effect of mercury on human health is unknown, but, if it is dangerous, many people will be harmed and the effect will continue to be felt because mercury will persist in the environment for years.[24]

The remedy preferred by no-growth futurists is the immediate institution of strict pollution controls and stabilization of population and industrialization for the long term. To these policy suggestions is added the hope that the damage to the ecological system and to human life is not already irreversible.

Population

No-growth futurists decry the current trend of population growth. It took 250 years for the world population to double from 0.5 billion people (in 1650) to 1 billion people (in 1900). If these rates of increase continue, the present world population of 3.6 billion people is expected to double in about 30 years.[25] To complicate the situation, the largest population increases take place in nonindustrialized areas which are beset by poverty and starvation. It is estimated that approximately one-third of the world's inhabitants are malnourished.[26]

Population has increased dramatically because the number of births exceed the number of deaths. Methods of controlling the diseases that previously wiped out entire populations are widely used. Superior methods of assisting during childbirth have significantly increased infant survival. Moreover, food production has increased because of the "green revolution." However, it is observed with consternation that there is a great difference between the amount and nutritive quality of food available in developed countries and in undeveloped countries.

According to no-growth futurists, the consequences of an exponential growth of population are several:

1. Food supplies will be strained even more than they are now, which will increase the number of starving people.

2. Condition 1. will worsen because more land will have to be diverted from agriculture and used for housing, waste disposal facilities, roads, power lines, and so on.

3. Pollution will increase because of condition 2.

4. Fresh water, which is necessary for maintaining ecological balance, will become scarce because of its use in irrigation and its pollution by industrial and human wastes.[27]

No-growth futurists estimate that there are 3.2 billion hectares of land potentially suitable for agricultural production. Approximately one-half are now under cultivation.[28] To prepare the remaining land for cultivation will require enormous outlays of capital. No-growth futurists cite the conclusion of the UN Food and Agricultural Organization that it is economically unfeasible to do so.[29]

It has been noted that the population is greatest in the poor nations of the world, whereas the industrial West has made significant strides toward a steady-state population. The continuation of this trend will widen the gap between rich and poor nations immeasurably. An offshoot of such a probability will be an intensification of political tensions within the starving nations and between rich and poor nations. It is unlikely that poorer nations will be able to battle successfully with rich nations. However, developed nations whose agricultural resources are in short supply might be motivated to fight agriculturally-rich nations on the pretense of defending the moral rights of starving nations. Certainly, history suggests that people are led into war under such pretenses.

Agriculture

As a population grows, the need for food increases. In response to the population boom, the green revolution dramatically increased agricultural production. In the United States, for example, agricultural output rose about 45 percent between 1949 and 1968.[30] This growth resulted from technological innovations in farm machinery, the development of high-yield grain varieties, and the use of inorganic fertilizers and synthetic pesticides.[31]

No-growth futurists seek to escalate and expand the green revolution. Nevertheless, they criticize some of the means of accelerated production and warn that agricultural growth, no matter how desirable, still runs up against the limits of a finite earth.

Specifically, the use of synthetic pesticides endangers health in ways that are not fully known. The case of DDT has already been mentioned. Inorganic fertilizers, if they do not present a health hazard, shorten the period of time in which land is usable. Arable land that has been abused by the use of inorganic fertilizers can turn into dust bowls.

Furthermore, the greater the dependence of agriculture on sophisticated machinery, the greater the cost of agricultural production because machinery becomes increasingly expensive as raw materials become scarcer. It is estimated that farmers achieved a 34 percent increase in production between 1951 and 1966 by increasing their annual expenditures on tractors by 63 percent, their expenditures on nitrate fertilizers by 146 percent, and their use of pesticides by 300 percent.[32] These costs were so high that only large farm companies could afford these investments. Small farmers were (and continue to be) forced out of business because they could not market their produce at competitive prices. If competition did not put small farmers out of business, high real estate taxes did. One of the unanticipated side effects of the green revolution is an increase in agricultural unemployment. In Mexico, agricultural production increased at an annual rate of 5 percent between 1940 and 1960. Nevertheless, the real income of the landless laborer decreased from $68 to $56 from 1950 to 1960.[33]

No-growth futurists, then, expect a greater concentration of agricultural production in the hands of large farmowners. However, as the cost of production continues to rise as a result of the high cost of capital investment in machinery, eventually agricultural production will decline. It will simply be too expensive to continue on a large scale. Of course, the need for food will lead people to continue growing food, but the high cost of machinery will reduce production.

Economy

No-growth futurists cite the fact that economic growth accelerated in the post-World War II period. They add disapprovingly that accelerated economic growth was centered in the industrial West, the result of which was a dramatic widening of the gap between rich and poor nations. Furthermore, as the consequences of exponential industrial growth evolve, the economic system will collapse.

The disapproval voiced by no-growth futurists about the economic future is supported by considerable independent research. E. J. Mishan suggests that continued economic growth in developed countries is ultimately deleterious to social well-being. The fruits of growth will not even "trickle down" to improve the lives of the lower classes because industrial management is concerned solely with profits and will produce only those goods that will generate the greatest profits.[34] Thus, the interests of the rich will be satisfied, whereas the interests of the poor and lower-middle classes will be ignored. In the housing industry, for example, upper-income housing is increasing, whereas low- and middle-income housing is decreasing.

The claim that the trickle-down thesis of classical economics is invalid is supported by studies of the economic distribution in the United States. Lester Thurow and Robert Lucas demonstrated that, during the years of economic growth between 1947 and 1970, the relative income distribution of various groups was essentially unchanged.[35] Another study by Peter Henle indicated that the income of male workers in the lowest fifth of the income scale declined, while the income of those in the highest fifth increased between 1958 and 1970.[36]

In general, economic studies, such as those made by Kenneth Boulding,[37] indicate that the free-market system does not adequately satisfy human needs because there is excessive duplication and insufficient production of important goods. Moreover, such studies corroborate the claim of no-growth futurists that the failure to consider the ecological consequences of industrial policies will eventually lead to economic chaos. The unstated assumptions underlying these conclusions are that the profit motive determines the course of production and the consumer does not know what he needs.

The General Goals of No-Growth Futurism

No-growth futurists are not optimistic that any measures will save world society. They merely suggest remedies that might rescue the world from self-destruction, if people have the will to use them. The following goals are set:[38]

1. The population should be stabilized. Industrial capital should be allowed to increase until the investment rate is equal to the depreciation rate.

2. To conserve nonrenewable resources, resource consumption per unit of industrial output should be reduced. This will give researchers time to find substitutes for depleted resources.

3. There should be a shift in economic interests from material production to service-oriented activities, such as education, medicine, and culture. This will reduce pollution and resource depletion and will improve the quality of life.

4. Pollution must be reduced.

5. Capital should be diverted from industrial to agricultural development.

6. More expenditures should be earmarked for the enrichment and preservation of the soil.

7. Through recycling, industrial waste should be reduced. Also, industrial production policies must be altered so that goods that are durable are produced.

Overriding all of these factors is the problem of the distribution of the world's wealth. Since a global society is desired, there must be a significant redistribution of food and economic power. No-growth futurists suggest that "the industrial parts of the world deliberately stop their industrial growth and possibly even 'shrink' somewhat, while the nonindustrialized world is allowed (and maybe helped) to grow economically to an acceptable, but not infinitely high, level."[39] If these changes are not forthcoming, it is claimed that social collapse and ecological disaster will be inevitable. If human beings survive, the chaotic aftermath will give way to a new dark age. If, on the other hand, the suggestions of no-growth futurists are followed, then a new golden age might emerge. An age in which self-development of the individual will flower. "The freedom from ever-increasing capital, that is, from more concrete, cars, dams, and skyscrapers, would make it possible for our great-grandchildren to enjoy solitude and silence." These are the words of Jorgen Randers and Donella H. Meadows, not mine.[40]

2. The Likely Consequences of Attempting to Institute a Steady State

The Consequences of No-Growth Policies

I maintain that the successful implementation of the policies of no-growth futurists will be politically harmful to nations of the first world. The USSR and the Chinese People's Republic will be strengthened. Since the United States, the Soviet Union, and China are the leading military powers in the world and since each of these nations seeks wide political influence, a strengthening of the position of the others (the Soviet Union and China) will have significant consequences for the future of the world. In this context, I consider the United States to be the most influential nation in the first world. Although European nations, such as France, West Germany, and Great Britain, and Asian nations, like Japan, follow independent courses of action, these nations are militarily and economically dependent on the United States. Therefore, a weakening of the position of the United States will weaken in various degrees, the positions of these nations.

At this juncture, I shall discuss the events that I think will occur if no-growth policies are implemented. I will not make evaluative judgments. However, after my theory of liberalism has been developed in Chapters 4 and 5, I will apply the theory to the practical world situation in Chapter 6. In Chapters 4 and 6, I will make evaluative judgments.

I do not imply that the Soviet Union and China are allies. It is obvious that Chinese leaders consider the Soviet Union to be the primary threat to their security.[1] Furthermore, the reasons for the conflict between China and the Soviet Union go beyond ideological disputes, although the breach is generally justified on theoretical grounds. The initial cause for the break was Mao Tze-tung's belief that the Soviet Union was not treating China as a great power deserving special foreign aid, a sharing of nuclear technology, and a part in decision making.[2] Subsequently, disputes arose over their mutual borders. China wanted to reoccupy territories acquired by czarist regimes. It was reasoned that these sparsely populated regions could provide an outlet for China's burgeoning population. The Soviet Union, however, refused to give up its czarist conquests.[3]

Despite the reality of the tension between the Soviet Union and China, both nations are ideologically opposed to the United States, that is, their political goals are antithetical to those of the United States. Even though détente between the Soviet Union and the United States and rapprochement between China and the United States have been established, there are good reasons to believe that friendlier relations do not signal an end to a fundamental hostility. The following passage from the World Communist Declaration of 1960 implies that the "international class struggle," in which the United States is considered to be the mainstay of the opposition, is to continue:

> . . . peaceful co-existence of countries with different social systems does not mean conciliation of the socialist and bourgeois ideologies. On the contrary, it means intensification of the struggle of the working class, of all the communist parties, for the triumph of socialist ideas. But ideological and political disputes between States must not be settled through war.[4]

Krushchev, the Russian leader generally credited with introducing an alleged liberalization of Soviet policy, made the following remark in a speech on January 6, 1961.

> There will be wars of liberation as long as imperialism exists, as long as colonialism exists. They are revolutionary wars. Such wars are not only permissible but inevitable . . . what should our attitude be to such uprisings? It should be most favourable.[5]

Although it is true that Soviet policy has softened since Stalin's death, the policies of the USSR toward the United States (opposing U.S. foreign policies in most cases), Cuba, Hungary, Czechoslovakia, Poland, and Afghanistan demonstrate that it still seeks to influence the political and military paths of foreign countries. Certainly, Soviet political action is invariably justified by the Soviet Union's commitment to international communism. Brian Crozier makes the following comment about the use of Marxist ideology in statements by Soviet officials:

> In international affairs, Russia's nationalistic and imperialistic invasion of Czechoslovakia is justified in the name of socialist internationalism. The same slogan presides over Moscow's attempts to regain

control over the international communist parties. . . . The ruling party justifies its monopoly of power on ideological grounds. If it abandoned the claims to ideological purity, it would be discarding the philosophical and indeed moral justification for that monopoly.[6]

China sees itself as a great power that must solve internal (industrial, agricultural, and military) growth problems before it can fulfill its destiny. This is partly a projection of precommunist nationalistic goals that are justified by reference to China's long cultural history. China is also a communist nation that believes that the Soviet Union can no longer lead the communist nations of the world because it has become a social-imperialist power and has revived capitalism.[7] As the self-proclaimed protector of the Marxist-Leninist tradition, China has embarked on a policy of industrial growth in order to build up its military strength and to meet challenges emanating from the Soviet Union and the United States.

Therefore, given the basic assumption of the Chinese leaders about world politics, they must give high priority both to improving China's ability to defend itself and to reducing the risk of attack. This has resulted, on the one hand, in the diversion of substantial resources to producing nuclear weapons and other modern arms, and, on the other hand, political moves aimed at keeping tension with the U.S.S.R. at a tolerable level, improving relations with the United States, and seeking to forestall trends toward militarism in Japan.[8]

That China has improved relations with the United States is not a sign that the fundamental ideological opposition between these nations has been overcome. Still, whereas China considers the threat from the Soviet Union to be imminent, the American threat is thought to have abated.

As for the United States, the Chinese probably expect that the trend of public opinion in this country in the wake of the unhappy Vietnam experience, together with Chinese success both in developing a nuclear deterrent and in cultivating better relations with the United States, will provide some assurance against any renewed U.S. military threat in the near future.[9]

Just as China's political philosophy leads the Chinese to pursue growth policies, the Soviet Union—in order to protect its Western borders, extend its political influence, and advance the Marxist-Leninist viewpoint—continues to pursue industrial and military growth. The Soviet Union is motivated by traditional attitudes and Marxist beliefs.

> In the field of industrialization, progress under Soviet communism has been immense. . . . From a Marxian viewpoint, equitable redistribution of income should have been the main objective. . . . However, the Soviet leaders were not only Marxists but also realistic nationalists who regarded Soviet power and prestige rather than distributive egalitarianism as the top priority. As a result, industrialization was focused on heavy industry and military preparedness as well as on specific programs in science and technology.[10]

The point of this discussion of the policies and ideologies of the Soviet Union and China is to demonstrate that these nations are embarked on international paths that conflict with those of the United States, a liberal nation, and its allies.

It is doubtful that the Soviet Union and China will be significantly affected by no-growth futurism. For the reasons I have indicated, multiple forces interact to form policy in the Soviet Union and China. These policies are concerned with industrial and military growth. To be sure, there are internal pressures in both nations to improve living conditions for ordinary citizens, but these pressures have not been sufficient to dislodge the goals of industrial and military growth from their primary positions in Chinese and Soviet planning.

In the Soviet Union, for example, peasant pressure against farm collectivism has led the government to permit farmers to devote some time to small, private plots of land and general unrest has led the government to broaden consumer choice.[11] Nevertheless, these changes have not altered the overall thrust of Soviet planning. Despite the desires of ordinary citizens, the problems of inadequate services and housing shortages remain severe, farm collectivism continues to be the dominant form of agriculture, and light industry is publicly owned. It has been concluded that "in the Soviet Union the government continues to determine the amount of available materials and manpower to be allocated to construction of heavy industry, space complexes, and military installations rather than of shops, motels, restaurants, and supermarkets."[12]

Since the death of Mao in 1976, China has embarked upon policies that were more responsive to the interests of citizens. Specifically, it has reversed the trends of the Cultural Revolution (1966-1969) by permitting the cultivation of private plots, moderating foreign policy, expanding foreign trade, and improving the economy.[13] Just as in the case of the

Soviet Union, however, there has not been a liberalization of the basic political system.

The conclusion I draw is that industrial and military growth probably will continue to be the major policies in these countries because moderating internal forces are not strong enough to alter fundamental policy. The situation is not the same in the United States because of the institutionalization of the freedoms of speech and press. A consequence of such institutionalization is the news media, educators, and authors are able to influence public policy. It is probable that the American reaction to the no-growth futurist criticisms of industrial growth policies will be to accept, however, tentatively, responsibility for creating problems and to seek, however halfheartedly, to redress them.[14]

There are some who will doubt that the media is as influential as I suggest. Using reasoning that was popular during the 1960s, it will be argued that military and industrial factions will prevent the government from responding to no-growth futurists. Supposedly, these factions will assume that industrial growth proceeds as usual. I believe that this sort of argument has already been refuted. To be sure, the military and industry are not impotent. In the fall of 1979, the American Senate amended the federal budget to provide for an increase in military spending of 40 billion dollars over the next three years.[15] This action was initially opposed by President Carter on the grounds that it was inflationary at a time of expected recession. However, when a revolution occurred in Iran and the Soviet Union invaded Afghanistan, Carter asked for greater military expenditures. This led many congressmen and political observers to protest that the President's measures far exceeded the real threat to world peace. In 1980, cold war rhetoric was revived with enthusiasm in the United States. Given the magnitude of the reaction to the alleged world crisis, Carter's actions must be viewed as a victory for the military. (The election of Ronald Reagan as President can also be interpreted as evidence of the influence of the military.) Similarly, oil interests have influenced Congress to the extent that it rejected a windfall profits tax proposed by President Carter. However, despite the continued influence of industry and the military, there is ample evidence that no-growth futurists have been heard. Many energy proposals made by the Carter administration to overcome the 1979-1980 oil crisis were consistent with central no-growth beliefs. Almost all commentators on energy assume that the oil crisis occurred, at least partially, because the supply of oil is being depleted at a fast rate. These commentators take it for granted that the American public must consume less oil. Consequently, they do not object to higher prices. (Liberals object to the windfall profits being made by oil companies, but not to higher prices.) President Carter's energy program sought, as no-growth futurists advise, to find alternate sources of energy.

As a consequence of the collision of these diverse forces—the military seeking growth, industry trying to increase profits in a steady *or* growing state, and experts and some politicians attempting to slow growth so that energy sources are available in the future—the American political machine will stall, or the policies that emerge will be halfhearted and contradictory. Such indecision or half-decision leads to the condition that I fear—a lessening of the political and economic power to the United States and other industrial nations. (It is too early to tell whether Ronald Reagan will have a consistent policy that he will be able to pass through Congress.)

In the developing world, energy-rich nations can be expected to improve their economic and political positions. Already, Middle East nations have benefited. Outside the United States, Japan, and Western Europe, there was widespread approval of the Organization of Petroleum-Exporting Countries (OPEC) oil policies in 1973 and 1979. And given the Western tradition of free speech and press, there was sympathy for the OPEC nations even in the nations adversely affected by OPEC oil price increases. As a result, OPEC received favorable settlements. A point that might be overlooked is that the West could have instituted a cold war. Not only was a peaceful line toward OPEC followed, but the United States also softened its support of Israel. It should be obvious that had the United States chosen a harder line, Israel could have been employed as a gadfly.

Whether or not the American course was wiser than the hard line alternative, the logic employed by those who sympathize with OPEC is questionable. The philosophical basis for approval of the Middle East position is that the United States has taken economic advantage of the Middle East for generations and that this injustice was rectified somewhat by the oil crisis. It was expected that a settlement favorable to the Middle East would be a start toward redistributing the world's wealth (one of the international goals of no-growth futurists). At the same time, it was hoped that the resultant higher price of oil would reduce consumption in the United States. However, the life of the average citizen in the Middle East has not substantially improved because most of the OPEC nations operate to the advantage of entrepreneurs. Even though the growth of energy consumption has slowed in the United States, oil consumption may rise again when (and if) the economy revives and production increases. An undesirable side effect of the energy crisis is that the argument for using pollution-intense energy sources has been given new life. Environmental concern has been, and probably will continue to be, a main casualty of recent oil crises in the United States.[16]

Another international goal of no-growth futurists—to provide food at reasonable prices to the undernourished masses of countries such as India—is probably unattainable.[17] Even if agriculturally rich nations distribute food to poor nations at low prices, they will not be heroically altruistic. National selfishness is too ingrained a political attitude. However, although no-growth futurists will not be able to achieve a more equitable distribution of food resources, they may, by the pressure they create, manage to erode the political power of the West.

On a national level, the emphasis of no-growth futurists is on restricting production and consumption and reducing pollution and population growth primarily through higher prices and taxes in the industrialized West. If such policies are successful, the burden of change most likely will be borne by the poor, the middle class, and, in the United States, racial minorities. This will be the case because the entrenched upper and upper-middle classes will be able to use their economic power to force the enactment of laws favorable to their interests. Thus, legislatures will probably approve higher prices on consumer products that deplete resources and degrade the environment and raise taxes across the board. Given the profit motive, industry will almost certainly aim production at wealthier customers. The automotive industry in the United States returned to producing gas-guzzling luxury cars rather than economical small cars once the oil crisis of 1973 was over. The same process took place in the area of housing. The average home built in 1977 retailed for more than $50.000.[18] The average house built in 1967 would have retailed for considerably less. This runaway price escalation cannot be explained solely by the increased cost of lumber and other building materials. It is directly related to decisions by builders to concentrate on richer customers.[19] The manufacture of large, energy-consuming automobiles is rapidly declining. However, the American consumer and the American automotive manufacturers resisted the introduction of smaller, energy-efficient cars for some time. Two severe energy crises were necessary to bring about desirable changes.

A statement by former President Carter indicates the extent to which the burden of conservation is placed on the middle and working classes. In the 1980 State of the Union address, Carter beseeched American workers to seek modest salary increases, while tolerating higher costs. He explicitly acknowledged that such action would erode the buying power of ordinary citizens, but claimed that it would be necessary to slow economic growth in the United States. (He did not make clear, however, that "ordinary citizens" are not "all citizens," merely those in the middle and working classes.) The result, Carter said, would be a reduction in the budgetary deficit, which would strengthen the American economic position. Although this might be the result, Carter's policy would burden the middle class and the poor, benefit the upper and upper-middle classes (as will be argued below), and encourage no-growth futurists who contend that growth is no longer feasible.

Across-the-board taxing is another means by which the interests of the upper and upper-middle classes would be favored at the expense of the middle and lower classes. The advocates of across-the-board taxing erroneously think that equal taxing is equitable taxing. "Equal taxing" means taxing everyone the same amount; "equitable taxing" means taxing fairly. There is no rational requirement that the latter entails the former. In fact, equal taxing would hamper the poor greatly and the rich to only a minor degree. Equal taxing would erode the buying power of the poor so that they could not purchase luxuries and eventually could not afford necessities. Higher taxes inconvenience the rich. But this is not the entire case. When tax-supported industrial incentives are tied to high tax policies, we find that many industries actually make higher profits than before. A well-known case in point is the recent history of the petroleum industry. Not only did the major oil companies make record profits during the oil embargo of 1973, but they sought legislation creating incentives to search for indigenous oil and to research methods of converting shale deposits into liquid form.[20] By 1980, they obtained a removal of price controls and weakened the windfall profits tax.

Why can industry make record profits even though the number of potential customers is reduced? Because there are large upper-middle and upper classes that can afford luxury items. Why are the members of these groups insulated from a general recession? Because they are the industrial managers, entrepreneurs, service agents, and investors whose incomes increase as prices rise.[21] This point cannot be overemphasized: the sheer size of the American economy ensures that many industries and people benefit from steepening recession and escalating inflation.

To be sure, during a period of economic stagnation many industries suffer. For example, the automotive industry today reports large losses. However, the government seeks to shield industry as much as possible. The federally-guaranteed loan to Chrysler Corporation is a case in point. It is the small industries, the middle and working classes, and the poor who bear the greatest burdens of economic stagnation.

In the next chapter, I will give the philosophical reasons why it is undesirable for particular classes to suffer during the period when a steady-state society is set.

No-growth futurists propose to meet the goals of pollution control by legally restricting certain industrial and consumer practices and by raising prices and taxes on pollution-intense products. If these measures are successful, once again the burden will be placed on the middle class, the lower class, and minorities. For example, the cost to industry of instituting controls will be passed on to the consumer in the form of price increases which of course will be more easily absorbed by the upper class than by the middle class, lower class, or minorities.

Population control is a goal of no-growth futurists that seems to be attainable in the industrial West. Statistics indicate that some nations are already approaching a steady-state population.[22] This has been achieved primarily by propagandizing the virtues of family planning. Unfortunately, the population explosion in poorer parts of the world seems less responsive to voluntary controls. If these trends continue, the gap between rich and poor nations will widen. This will increase international disputes.

Why No-Growth Policies Produce Undesirable Consequences

The recommendations of no-growth futurists can be generally characterized as follows: international solutions are imbued with a moral idealism that runs up against the reality of social relations, and national solutions unintentionally favor the rich. Requiring the industrialized West to act altruistically in redistributing the world's material and agricultural wealth is exactly the sort of idealism that warrants the classic charge leveled against academics—that they live in ivory towers and are incapable of offering practical advice in moments of crisis. It should be said that nations or groups attempt to conduct social dealings on an international and national level to their own advantage. National or group interest is modified only when it is in the long-range interest of the acting nation or group to do so. In other words, power and rational self-interest dictate the direction of social relations. There are exceptions to this practice, but they are few. Furthermore, nations and groups within nations myopically see their long-range interests. Therefore, to suggest that nations act altruistically toward other nations or give up a significant part of their national autonomy for the general good is quixotic. As I have said, the real effect of these policies would be a decline in the pursuit of self-interest by free world nations to the advantage of communist powers. The free world would not sacrifice their self-interest entirely, but enough so that communist countries would be significantly aided.

Nevertheless, if international and national policies were governed by rationality, programs based on moral idealism would be beneficial. That is, if people were capable of perceiving long-range possibilities and were capable of modifying their desires accordingly, then people might choose to share with the poor of other nations and to grant greater authority to the United Nations. But if people were rational, then racial integration in the United States would have been realized decades ago, Russian authors would not be censored and imprisoned for criticizing the government, and a fair Middle East peace would be a reality.

In sharp contrast to the moral idealism of no-growth recommendations on an international level, the proposed solutions to national problems are shortsightedly pragmatic. They often satisfy industrial interests. To be sure, this is not their intention, nor do industrialists desire a steady-state society. Industry would accept a reduction in material consumption only as long as prices could be raised and tax incentives for future industrial investment were ensured. The long-range consequence of national no-growth policies would most likely be an exacerbation of class conflicts as the buying power of the poor and the middle class were eroded.

How a Steady-State World is to be Established

The principal writings of the no-growth futurists came as a bombshell. Although many social scientists were skeptical of no-growth claims, many liberals, at least in the United States, bought the thesis. Propaganda had taught them that "small is good and big is bad." People were urged to walk or ride bicycles rather than drive cars. They were advised to lower their heating systems in the winter and their cooling systems in the summer. The media gave a great deal of attention to the many solar heating pilot projects that emerged. "No more Nukes" became the cry of middle-aged and young liberals.

Overall, no-growth futurism produced a "return to nature" mentality. Many people developed a desire to run away from urban life with its squalor, crowding, and crime. There also arose a hatred of government for supposedly being too big to respond to the desires of citizens, too mendacious in announcing policies, and too much the tool of industry and the military.[23]

No-growth futurists employ two methods of promoting their goals: first, they seek to propagandize their beliefs through education and public demonstrations, and, second, they change their own life styles.

It is doubtful that public demonstrations will be effective. Political demonstrations were unsuccessful in attaining *desired* goals in the 1960s when they were larger, more emphatic, and had greater support than demonstrations have today. Being new and exciting in the 1960s, demonstrations became a fad. But fads die, and demonstrations lost their popularity when they became familiar, their targets more controversial, and their expression violent. They have left a bad taste in the mouth of the public and are no longer novel. Demonstrations can be successfully revived only if demonstrators convince bystanders that the issues at hand are crucially important and that the consequences of inaction will be devastating.

Education of the public probably would not be effective in the time allotted by no-growth futurists. As will be seen, time is a crucial factor, and no-growth futurists claim that it is in short supply. Education is a slow process: proponents of a new thesis must meet objections raised by the defenders of the status quo; once a new attitude is inculcated in people's minds, it takes time for practice to follow belief.

Finally, it is improbable that the changes in life style advocated by no-growth futurists could bring about a steady-state society. If the no-growth thesis is correct, social disaster is approaching at an *exponential* rate. Actual changes in life style among no-growth advocates is taking place *arithmetically*. That is, single individuals are slowly and gradually being added to the no-growth corps. However, an exponential increase in the number of people who will alter their life styles is necessary in order to counteract the exponential increase in problems. Furthermore, no-growth behavior must be adopted by other nations. Population control, for example, is required more in the developing world than in the United States and Western Europe. It is also desirable, if no-growth futurists are correct, in China. Finally, an industrial slowdown and a reduction in pollution could not be effected by individual citizen action. These goals must be adopted by big business and governments throughout the developed world.

I am attempting here to underscore a significant complaint: no-growth futurists have not advanced a realistic plan for establishing a steady-state society. This renders their work suspect. It is always possible to recommend social changes that would improve people's lives. The problem is to devise means by which the power of entrenched factions, who have an interest in maintaining the status quo, can be neutralized and by which the majority of citizens can be aroused to action. I have heard academic planners suggest that many significant social and economic problems in the United States could be solved by a political rearrangement of the country into fewer states. Supposedly, such political reconstruction would make the most efficient use of demographic and economic divisions. Even if this plan would in theory bring about the desired result, it would never be implemented because the economic, political, and social groups whose members benefit from the present arrangement would fight the change with every ounce of their power. Ordinary citizens, on the other hand, are too easily swayed by the authority of established classes to heed the advice of educators. Even if ordinary citizens were convinced by argument, they would not have the stamina to wage the long Constitutional battle that would be inevitable if the political structure of the country were to be altered.

The institution of a steady-state society would require as much effort and would be confronted by as potent an opposition as would restructuring the United States. Moreover, the steady-state movement would have to obtain the acquiescence of the first world, the communist world, and the third world. Given the practical difficulties alone, the establishment of a steady-state society would be impossible. If I believed the predictions of no-growth futurists, I would despair for the future of humankind.

I have presented two arguments in this chapter: first, that any attempts to bring about a steady-state society probably would be deleterious to the first world and, secondly, that the establishment of a steady-state society is not feasible. If these claims seem paradoxical, they are only apparently so. I have stated that no-growth futurists can have a sufficient impact in the United States and Western Europe to undermine policy-making in these areas which could swing political power to the communist world and third world. However, they will never have enough influence to overcome entrenched classes anywhere, and as a result a steady-state society will never be realized.

The Psychology of No-Growth Futurism

If my claims are correct, the reader may wonder why no-growth futurism is popular among liberals, particularly educators, writers, artists, and other intellectuals. The answer lies in a psychological attitude that has evolved in this century which condones a reduction in the power of the liberal nations of the world, especially the United States. How deeply ingrained this attitude is in such countries as France and West Germany is uncertain, but it is deeply held in the United States and Great Britain.

Two beliefs that support this attitude are that human beings have a right to complete self-development and that this right is denied to people by the self-centered acts of those who have economic, social, and political power. These beliefs form a core axiom of classical liberalism (which will be explored in detail later). That no-growth futurists adopt this axiom is not always articulated, nor is it always realized that it is a cornerstone of classical liberalism. This axiom was the basis for Marx's moral outrage at the flagrant abuse of laborers by industrial management and government. Marx was indignant because the human rights of the working class were not championed by social institutions claiming to be economically and politically neutral (for example, the organized church). Later generations of liberals (hereafter called contemporary liberals) were converted to the cause of labor and shared with Marxists a distrust of social and political institutions that was based on the unwillingness of these institutions, industrialists, and the upper classes to better the life of the working classes.

More recently, contemporary liberals have fought for the rights of racial minorities in the United States and the poor in third world nations. The basis for their interest in these groups is the same as before: the belief that human beings have a *right* to complete self-development. Again, liberals believe that the self-centered acts of those who have economic, social, and political power thwart the opportunities of the oppressed classes. The villains in this case are political and social institutions as before, and, for the first time, first world nations, especially the United States. These countries are the object of the scorn previously heaped on large industrial corporations.

In the consciousness of no-growth futurists, then, is an antipathy toward first world nations, political and social institutions, and first world values. Since first world nations are concerned with material consumption and the accumulation of wealth, these interests are condemned. Since urban life has been the center of economic development in the West, urban life is condemned. (There are other reasons why urban life is condemned.)

Corresponding to this hostility toward the first world is a favorable attitude toward any sociopolitical force that opposes the first world. Just as the communist government in Russia had only to oppose the West to gain the sympathy of Western liberals in the 1930s and 1940s, the Ayatollah Khomeini had only to oppose the Shah of Iran, who was supported by the United States, to gain the allegiance of contemporary liberals. It was sufficient for liberals in the 1930s and 1940s to believe that Western governments oppressed labor and supported capitalists to sympathize with Joseph Stalin's regime in Russia. When confronted with the evidence that Stalin's government violated the civil and human rights of Russian citizens, they either denied the evidence or rationalized it on the grounds that excesses were necessary to effect a revolution that would eventually promote human rights. Today, there are liberals who reason similarly on behalf of the Ayatollah Khomeini's regime in Iran, although after American hostages were taken in Iran, support for the religious revolution declined.

At the root of the reasoning applied in these and many other cases is the assumption that everything can be rigidly categorized as either good or bad. If an institution is demonstrably bad, that which opposes it is good. This sort of analysis fails to take into account the fact that there are many alternatives and that there are degrees of goodness and badness. The Western nations may not have been good in the 1930s and 1940s, but Stalin's Russia may not have been either. In fact, it may have been considerably worse. Furthermore, although the United States may not have been ideally good, it may have been fairly good. The same reasoning applies in the case of the Ayatollah Khomeini. The Shah undoubtedly violated human rights, but so has Khomeini. Is one government better than the other? Possibly, but the change of government has been too recent for us to draw a conclusion. It is sufficient to note that neither government is entitled to receive an unqualified endorsement from those who are interested primarily in promoting human and civil rights.

As we have seen, the psychology of no-growth futurism includes an antipathy toward first world governments and social and political institutions because they have produced an environment in which the human and civil rights of downtrodden classes have not been fully realized. The tendency of contemporary liberals and of no-growth futurists is to conclude that the first world is bad and to evaluate those opposed to it as good. The evidence that the USSR has violated human rights is so strong that contemporary liberals no longer view that nation as a moral alternative to the first world. Nevertheless, there is sympathy for other communist nations and enormous sympathy for third world nations. There is no evidence demonstrating the superiority of these nations and their social institutions. Contemporary liberals blithely dismiss the fact that the governments of these nations are not based on democratic principles: to demand democracy is to be provincial. They claim that democracy has not worked to the advantage of racial minorities in the United States and, hence, cannot be considered an ideal form of government. Those who hold these views do not demand evidence that the interests of lower classes are satisfied in the third world or communist nations—they merely assume it. They apply "black-white" logic.

This logic is naive and certainly not all no-growth futurists adopt it.

Nevertheless, it accounts for the popularity of no-growth futurism, at least partially. There is simply an eagerness to join the bandwagon in pursuit of a new ideal. The new ideal seems desirable because it has not been sullied by contact with reality.

The purpose of discussing this psychology is to remind the reader that social reform, however attractive, is not easy to effect without creating human dislocations. People ought not to rush into social revolution unless they have prepared for dangers and have established that the proposed reforms are better than the established system. Caution is being expressed here, not conservatism.

3. Counterpoint: The Moral Implications of No-Growth Futurism and Doubts About the Empirical Claims of No-Growth Futurists

In this chapter, the main arguments of the book will be outlined, and the philosophical and moral theory on which opposition to no-growth futurism is based will be sketched. In the last chapter, it was argued that the issue of human rights is ignored by no-growth futurists when they consider national problems. The argument was given general expression so that readers could accept or reject it regardless of their moral or political connections. In the first section of this chapter, human rights will be related specifically to liberal theory. In subsequent chapters, a particular version of liberalism will be enlarged and defended. In the second section of this chapter, reasons for rejecting the no-growth claim that industrial society has run its course will be given. The first section considers philosophical matters; the second delves into empirical evidence. In the final section, reasonable policies for the future will be outlined in light of the earlier conclusions.

The Moral Objections to No-Growth Futurism

Even if the warning of no-growth futurists about industrial and economic growth were warranted and a steady-state society could be established, there would be moral reasons for rejecting the no-growth thesis. If the plans of no-growth futurists were implemented, the classical goal of Western liberalism would be lost. That goal is to maximize personal freedom in order to maximize personal development and happiness. There has been a trend in this century toward making personal liberty a legal right. For the first time in history, the commitment to individual liberty has been more than the rhetoric of emperors, commissars, or parliaments. In the United States, at least, it seems to be a reality. The modern champions of personal liberty or individual rights were (and are) liberals who fought for *civil rights*. Most people do not realize that the policies of no-growth futurists pose a threat to the attainment of the traditional liberal goal.

The relationship between the theory of liberalism and liberal government must be clarified. I will discuss primarily the theory as it evolved in the West, especially in Great Britain and the United States. In this section, the term "liberalism" is used in the general sense to refer to a theory of government. Correspondingly, the United States is considered a liberal state, as are France and Great Britain.

The theory of liberalism implies that each person has a moral right (in the United States this is expressed as a constitutional civil right) to maximal liberty. This can be achieved only by maximizing social and economic opportunity. This proviso of liberalism is often overlooked, but it is essential for understanding the direction of the civil rights movement in this century. Industrial growth has been the means by which economic and social opportunity has been obtained.

An ancillary belief of liberalism is that material well-being is a necessary condition of personal fulfillment. That is, material well-being is the means through which people develop diverse interests. Consequently, the social environment must be such that all citizens have the opportunity for economic development. This amendment to liberalism was fully formulated by Adam Smith in the eighteenth century. One hundred and fifty years later, another premise was added to liberalism: government must provide social and economic assistance to people on the lowest classes of society so that they can overcome social barriers. This last-stated addition to the liberal thesis caused the most trauma among liberals and is the raison d'être of the twentieth century civil rights movement. This theoretical amendment was originally suggested in the later writings of John Stuart Mill and articulated by T. H. Green.[1] One of the most dramatic chapters in the history of liberalism concerns the labor movement. The evolving liberal consciousness supported organized labor in its fight for political recognition. As labor achieved its goals of increased wages and improved working conditions, the worker found protection from the vagaries of the market. Unintentionally, however, socialism was broached because the freedom of the market was compromised. The threat of socialism was diminished by expanding markets since increases in labor costs were made up by increases in gross income. The success of capitalism in averting the socialist threat is brought out by the fact that there has been no significant redistribution of wealth in the United States in the last forty years.[2] Comparable statistics can be cited for England, France, and West Germany.

The means by which capital expanded its markets was technological innovation, which led to higher rates of production, quicker and more efficient means of distributing goods through better transportation systems, and increased consumption brought about in part by advertising. Stated succinctly, the liberal economic system survived primarily by accelerating and expanding industrial growth, and, at the same time, satisfying labor's desire for increased wages.[3]

Given the relative freedom of capital and labor, they are engaged in nonmortal conflict. Labor incessantly seeks to increase its advantages; capital doggedly tries to maintain, if not increase, its income. Government mediates to protect the social structure and to ensure the survival of all combatants.

If we view the history of the labor movement from the standpoint of the philosophies of the actors, it can be said that business advocates justified their position through the original liberal theory, labor invoked Mill's amended version of liberalism, and government acted as a mediator to preserve the political system.

Today, the liberal movement, beyond ensuring the preservation of the balance of power between labor and business, seeks to expand economic and social opportunities for others. In countries such as the United States, members of minorities and unskilled workers have not yet organized strong factions capable of combating established factions (capital, labor, and so on). In European nations, the goal of liberals is to redistribute wealth since the upper classes there are more entrenched than they are in the United States. In short, the goal of liberalism—maximal social and economic opportunity for self-development—has not been attained.

At this point, the moral objection to no-growth futurism can be articulated. If economic and industrial growth is halted at any cost without regard for the individual, then the liberal commitment to maximal personal freedom will be lost. For example, no-growth futurists condone increasing prices as a means of reducing oil consumption, but those who are victimized by such policies as this are the middle class, the working class, and the poor, which in the United States include minorities, recent immigrants, the poorly educated, and, as always, small farmers. It is surprising that contemporary liberals, whose forebearers mobilized the labor movement and the twentieth-century civil rights movement, are willing to halt industrial growth and protect the environment at the expense of these very groups. What liberals often overlook in their enthusiasm for a new crusade is that the proposed means of resolving the problem at hand conflict with old goals. In fact, if industrial growth is sufficiently hampered without accompanying social change, the social advantages that have been won for the individual in this century will be lost. Paraphrasing Marx, people will fall from the middle class into the exploited proletariat in increasing numbers.

In order to emphasize the significance of what might be lost, I shall place the liberal concern for the individual in perspective. Throughout most of history, governments have been concerned with the "general welfare" or the "general happiness." In practice, however, governments have mainly ignored the interests of the people and responded to the whims of rulers, even though the rulers have invariably claimed to be seeking the general welfare. The great Western political revolutions of the modern era placed in political power people who promised to make the general welfare the real, as well as the ideal, goal of government. Furthermore, the method of obtaining political office by general elections was thought to ensure the attainment of the general welfare. In practice, only those rich enough to advance themselves and those who were capable of aligning themselves with others of like interest in groups or factions could influence the electorate and the legislature. Although revolutions made governments responsive to a greater variety of interests, governments continued to serve only *special* interests. Those who were too poor or too weak to form factions were denied the advantages of social life. In effect, they gained nothing from the overall prosperity but suffered most from economic depression. These people were invariably denied the rights granted to individuals by constitutions and had to serve most strenuously during times of war and crisis. Twentieth-century liberals have been identified by their goal of making governments serve the interests of all people—even faction*less* people. That is why liberals in the United States have fought for the disfranchised—blacks, American Indians, migrant farm workers, and people accused of committing crimes.

The goal of this book is to prevent liberals from abandoning the pursuit of the rights of individuals.

It might be thought that the goals of no-growth futurists can be altered to include a national redistribution of wealth and the retention of power among the nations of the free world. But even this will not work because there is no possibility that economic, social, and political leaders can be convinced to act fairly. Selfishness is too ingrained in the human personality for this to happen.[4] Those in power will scheme and rationalize to protect their advantages until they die. The majority of people will rouse themselves to perceive the distress of others only in a catastrophic situation such as war. The social collapse imagined by no-growth futurists will proceed slowly and insidiously. By their own admission, the collapse will not be perceived by the general public until it is too late to take remedial measures. Once again, cigarette smoking can be used as an analogy. The worst effects of smoking are usually perceptible only after twenty or thirty years. When the damage to the lungs or heart is felt, most people can give up cigarettes, but by then damage is irreversible. Just as most people were not persuaded to give up cigarette smoking even after a massive publicity campaign informing the public of the consequences of smoking, no-growth futurists cannot expect to convince the world's social and political leaders to share wealth nationally or internationally. The point of the analogy is that, if most people do not change their behavior when they obtain hard scientific evidence, they will not change their behavior in response to speculative sociopolitical claims.

In light of the impracticality of no-growth recommendations, I believe that a policy of industrial growth should be continued so that (1) the poor obtain a fair share of the wealth within nations and (2) the ideals of the free world are upheld. I contend that industrial growth should continue because inequities exist in society now, whereas predictions about the future are uncertain. There are always unknown conditions and unanticipated factors that may alter the path of the future. Even if every current indicator suggested that social disaster were ahead, we could only predict a *probable* disaster. In the actual situation, we know inequities exist; there is no reason to expect that society will adjust fairly and peacefully to a steady-state society. Therefore, it is best to proceed as if a steady-state society were not necessary, because continual growth will satisfy, at least, the interests of many downtrodden people in this generation. And social disaster may not occur.

The reasoning here is not that we must act on the hope that the future will be better regardless of the evidence but on the hope that the future will be better when there is no reasonable expectation that a policy can be devised to bring about a better future and when there are immediate gains to be obtained by continuing to follow present policy.

Fortunately, the situation is not so bad as no-growth futurists contend. It will be argued that their predictions are unwarranted because many of their empirical claims are false.

Has Industrial Society Run Its Course?

As stated earlier, industrial technology, rather than being inherently deleterious to social well-being, is the practical expression of the scientific temperament and the everyday means by which human ingenuity works to gain mastery over a hostile environment. A significant reason for the superiority of Western culture has been the elevation of the scientific temperament. From Ancient Greece through the Renaissance to the twentieth century, the scientific attitude has imbued life with confidence and vigor, qualities that have spilled over into the arts and literature. The result has been the creation of a progressive society that has been unmatched in the rest of the world. Those who possess the scientific temperament search relentlessly and fearlessly for explanations, confident that all processes can be understood and that ways can be found to make the environment serve humankind.

It is taken, as people in the West generally have taken it, that comfortable social living—that is, an environment in which food is readily available, shelter adequate, and means of communication and transportation sophisticated—is a necessary, although not sufficient, condition of personal and social well-being. Without minimal comfort, people cannot develop social virtues beyond their primitive expressions. It is because scientific technology provides essential social comforts that I oppose the present tendency to downgrade industrial society.

I am not merely trying to conserve a glorious past. No-growth futurists simply have not proved that the capacity of the natural environment to provide for growth through technological innovation has been exhausted. In fact, the evidence of history indicates that technological innovation is the very means by which the present energy-environmental crisis can be overcome.

Certain events give the no-growth thesis superficial plausibility. The recurring energy crisis has led people to believe that the world is running out of natural resources. The persistent recessions of the 1970s have raised doubts about the fundamental health of Western economic systems. Contrary to known economic laws, recent recessions have been accompanied by rising inflation. The unorthodox path of economic downturns suggests, as the no-growth futurists claim, that capital investment is more intensive regardless of the economic cycle, thereby making escalating inflation unavoidable. If this opinion is correct, the future of Western economies is indeed uncertain.

In opposition to this view, it can be stated that the reason for the oil crises has not been that the world supply of oil is running out. Rather, the energy crisis of 1973 was politically motivated by the desire of OPEC nations to embarrass the West, especially the United States, for its support of Israel. Furthermore, the failure of Western nations to prepare for shortages demonstrated the lack of political wisdom in light of the fact that *the use of oil as a political and economic lever against the West had been predicted by experts for some time.*[5] There is also considerable evidence that oil companies in the United States, rather than running out of domestic supplies of oil, consciously shifted to buying oil from the Middle East because Middle East oil was cheaper. This led to a reduction in exploration for new oil in the United States and eventual dependence on Middle East oil.[6]

When speaking of the causes of the oil crisis of 1979, one must be more cautious because its full implications have not yet been felt. Some of the factors involved are the following: (1) The revolution in Iran led to production shortfalls; (2) in order to raise prices, other oil-rich nations refused to increase the amount of oil extracted from the ground; and (3) the major U.S. oil companies adopted policies that permitted them to raise prices. The implication is that economic and political factors have been largely responsible for the recent oil crisis. Although this may not be absolutely certain, the facts themselves are not in doubt, and the facts contravene the no-growth claims.

There are reasons to believe that no-growth futurists are also incorrect in claiming that the supply of fossil fuels and mineral resources is being depleted at an exponential rate. Recent studies show that resources generally will be available for centuries to come. Among the highly available resources are coal, iron, lead, chromium, manganese, and zinc. Among the resources that may be in short supply are oil, natural gas, mercury, and gold. The resources that receive the greatest attention are energy resources, such as oil and natural gas. Although the prognosis concerning their availability is not optimistic, two factors should alleviate most fears. First, the technology for developing substitutes is available. Synthetic fuels fall in this category. (Environmental problems can be solved by technological innovation.) Second, esoteric technologies (such as solar energy and geothermal energy) are being developed. A full discussion of energy sources is taken up in Chapter 8. The case of mineral resources is considerably brighter. Most of the resources in the crust of the earth are virtually inexhaustible, and those that are in short supply can be replaced by substitutes. For example, paper and plastic can replace tin in cans; plastics substitute for lead in building construction; nickel and zinc replace chromium in plating iron. Mineral resources are discussed in Chapter 9.

The overriding factor that should assure us that resources will be available in the future is that predictions of available resources have always erred on the negative side. The supply of actual resources has far exceeded predicted amounts because (1) research methods are crude, (2) predictions do not account for technological innovation, and (3) industry does not consider it economically sound policy to ensure resource supplies beyond a twenty-year period. These claims are discussed in Chapters 8 and 9.

There is a great deal of evidence to suggest that the recent energy crises were not caused by the West running up against a limited environment. Political uncertainty, in which governments do not have the will to make hard choices, is a significant cause of economic crisis. In the United States, for example, the government has not limited the use of foreign oil so that its import-export ratio is brought into balance. It has not legislated to force oil companies to resume large-scale exploration for indigenous oil and natural gas. It has not balanced its budget or placed strong price-wage restrictions on industry and labor. (These measures are only examples of what might be done to better the situation.) Furthermore, the United States is still suffering a hangover from its Vietnam misadventure. Not only did the cost of that war contribute to inflation, but the suspected mendacity of the government in pursuing the war led to a loss of public confidence which today prevents the government from taking strong measures. Other factors that contribute to the economic crises will be discussed later, but one of them is *not* that natural resources are running out. It is true that some resources are in short supply, but many of these shortages are temporary and, in cases of resources that will no longer be available, substitutes can be found.

Rationality and the Future

In this section, I will sketch the general path I believe society should take in order to overcome contemporary problems. I will not develop proofs for my opinion here, since I want only to alert the reader to the direction of my thinking. In subsequent chapters, the hard reasoning will be provided.

Nothing that has been said in criticism of no-growth futurism implies that the world is proceeding into the future sanely and safely. I believe that no-growth futurists are right in claiming that overpopulation and pollution intensification endanger the future. (Of course, many others have said the same thing. My disagreement is with the unique claim of no-growth futurists—that industrial society is obsolete.) Here I will acknowledge that population should be stabilized and pollution reduced. The difference in my viewpoint is that I believe change can occur gradually without disaster, whereas the no-growth futurists think that catastrophy is imminent.

Besides overpopulation and pollution, the supply of raw materials is one of the major problems we face. Some resources may be depleted in the near future, and others may be unavailable for political reasons. Invariably, cartels such as OPEC benefit those who are connected with them but hurt everyone else. In general, supplies of raw materials should be made to flow freely. New supplies of minerals in short supply and new sources of energy should be found; those resources that have been depleted should be replaced. This should be accomplished without degrading the environment.

Rationality and Industrial Future

Rational policy in industrial development requires, I believe, that means be devised to reduce consumption of the raw materials that may be depleted. Oil is a fossil fuel whose long-range availability is uncertain. Whether oil is in short supply because it is actually running out or it is being withheld from the market for economic and/or political reasons, it ought to be conserved. If the supply is being depleted, conserving oil will provide the time we need to find substitutes. If, on the other hand, the production of oil is being controlled by a cartel, oil exploration should be intensified so that the sources of this energy source be diversified. During the period of exploration, oil should be used sparingly. Similar policies should be developed to deal with other scarce resources.

Rational industrial policy requires that considerable effort be expended to develop new supplies of energy. I might add that the health of an industrial state is measured by the extent to which it searches for innovative ways of producing goods. Japan, with minimal natural resources, is flourishing economically because its industry, following the urgings of government, relentlessly seeks to apply technological innovation to production. (Social factors contribute to Japan's economic well-being as well.)

Despite my support for continued industrial development and growth, I maintain that industrial pollution ought to be controlled. Industrial spokesmen argue that pollution restrictions may produce permanent industrial stagnation and economic recession. This strikes me as an overstatement. The causes of the recession in the United States and Western Europe in the late 1970s and early 1980s are many. Pollution restrictions hamper industrial development, but they do not prevent it.

New, clean energy sources can be discovered through governmental and industrial research. Methods of converting coal and shale should be pursued. Solar energy should be studied and utilized at the earliest possible moment because it provides clean, inexhaustible energy. Finally, nuclear power research ought to be closely monitored. As Barry Commoner has pointed out, the environmental consequences of nuclear power are uncertain and potentially destructive.[7] Nuclear energy will be discussed in detail in Chapter 8.

As it will be argued later, the use of other nonrenewable resources presents dangers and options similar to those described above. Barry Commoner has said that the industrywide substitution of synthetic materials for natural materials (for example, plastic for wood, artificial sweeteners for sugar, polyester for wool, insecticides for plant rotation, etc.) was exactly the wrong choice.[8] It has resulted in the depletion of natural resources and the poisoning of the environment. I will not go as far as Commoner. In some cases, synthetic materials have been successfully substituted for resources in short supply. Insecticides, for example, have saved many thousands of people from starvation. Despite these disagreements, I believe that the side effects of using synthetic materials should be considered before they are widely used.

On an international level, rational planning is currently impossible because there is no organization that has the political power to control economic and social forces. The march toward rational worldwide planning is desirable because the exponential development of communication and transportation systems has laid the practical foundation for "one world." However, given human myopia, social recognition of this fact lags behind the reality. Convincing nations to implement *immediately* fair international practices is simply impossible.

Fair international practices are those in which resources, technology, goods, and wealth are distributed according to uniform standards. These standards should be developed rationally so that the interests of all those who participate in the distribution system are considered. For example, resources are generally extracted from some developing nations and fabricated in developed nations. Those who profit most from the use of these resources are the developed nations. The reason for this is that the developed nations have the power to arrange production processes to their advantage. The developing nations would like to receive greater economic rewards for their natural resources. A fair practice would take this desire into account and balance the conflicting interests. This problem will be discussed in greater detail in Chapter 6.

Although human beings are not ready to institute fair international practices, they might tolerate a modification of the pursuit of national self-interest as rationality seeps over into international policies. If this occurs, rich nations will share technological know-how, financial aid, and food with other nations *as long as they receive political compensation.* (See the section on liberal policies in the third world in Chapter 6.)

Seepage that produces some degree of rationality in international affairs requires that the pursuit of national self-interest includes provisions for reducing pollution and population and preserving natural resources. These policies would not be expected to replace the traditional fight for economic and political superiority. To hope for the latter would be collapsing into academic idealism. However, just as fear of nuclear war led to coexistence through détente, constant pressure might lead national leaders to seek to preserve the ecosphere.

Rationality, Population, and Land Preservation

Population control should be adopted as a means of preventing starvation and the intensification of pollution and of preserving land for agricultural use. Agricultural production should be increased so that food can be provided for the malnourished masses.

Population control must be achieved by different means in different places. In the liberal West, governments cannot directly enforce family planning without violating fundamental individual rights (*civil rights* in the United States, *human rights* internationally). Fortunately, because of the strides already made by the West in controlling population, individual rights need not be threatened. In the developing world, this may not be the case. Given the severity of the problem, it would be realistic to tolerate stringent birth control policies in some nations. If such measures jar our liberal consciences, we must remember that a "clear and present danger" exists, and, in such moments, survival takes precedence over personal freedom.

Land preservation and the cultivation of arid land ought to be made priorities in most nations. Although commentators disagree about the future availability of land, empirical evidence supports the claim that land for cultivation is not running out provided that population control is instituted.[9] Once again, the means by which more land can be made agriculturally usable is through technological innovation. It is technological innovation that has been largely responsible for the green revolution of the post-World War II years.[10] Similar results can be expected in the future.

Practicality and Rationality

Earlier I stated that no-growth solutions to the current energy-environmental crisis are mortally infected with academic idealism and romanticism. The same charge might be leveled against me for proposing that pollution control and industrial monitoring be intensified in the West. It could be countered that business interests have too much political influence and too little foresight to allow restrictions to be imposed on immediate profit making. It is unlikely that industrialists can be made to change their tune. Politicians cannot be forced to serve the general welfare rather than General Motors—their influence can be modified only by widespread social and political activism. Nonetheless, I believe that there is hope for the future if intellectual leaders use their power wisely. I am not predicting that society will survive the current crisis; I am only claiming that disaster is not inevitable and that means exist for preserving industrial society that do not require a change in human nature. Survival can be achieved by revising social goals.

Standing in the way of a shift in our priorities are (1) the propaganda employed by selfish interests and (2) the lassitude of the masses. The former can be counteracted by a zealous intellectual community. The latter exists because people have become convinced that government and social structures are too large and unmanageable to respond to citizen pressure. Ironically, no-growth futurists, who desire to bring about social change, contribute to the feeling of hopelessness by the very gloominess of their predictions. Is it any wonder that the ordinary citizen luxuriates in self-involvement? However, just as citizens were aroused to fight the wars of this century, they can be awakened to take part in the less dangerous, more rewarding enterprise of preserving the ecosphere. This will require that intellectuals adjust their message and try to convince people that they can affect society.

My interpretation of the current crisis is that it is not totally different from past social crises. We are at a low point, but we have the potential to survive and arrive at a new period of (relatively) untroubled growth. Because we live in an evolutionary world where the past is never repeated, this crisis is unique, just as every crisis is. It is exceptional because the refinement of industrial output produces greater fallout. By emphasizing the dangers of industrial development, we sometimes forget that industrial use is so effective that its rational employment can bring about great social advances. Therefore, if society makes the wrong choices, the effects can be more disastrous than in the past but if society makes the right choices, success can be greater than ever before. It is not uncommon for each generation to believe that its experience signals an irreversible trend. During periods of prosperity, people are resolutely optimistic; during a depression, they are unrelievedly pessimistic. The truth is that evey period has positive and negative potential. The job of intellectuals is to arouse people to overcome dangers by picking up the threads of promise.

It might be argued that by requiring that rationality and intelligence overcome selfishness, I am involved in a self-contradiction. It might be said that, if people are selfish, then rational intellectuals are selfish as well. To this criticism I reply that intellectuals can be "rationally self-interested," whereas others are less likely to be so. What distinguishes the intellectual community, when it functions effectively, is that its members take into account the interests of others, are capable of long-range planning, and can postpone immediate gratification. The fundamental *justification* for their acts may be fulfillment of self-interest, but the actual *practice* of social affairs will endorse fair sharing and altruism. Altruism for its own sake is the only traditional moral value that I would rule out as a motivation.

The Major Thesis

It is my contention that liberal morality requires the continuation of industrial growth so that the rights of individuals are satisfied. No-growth futurism stands in the way of the achievement of this goal. I believe that no-growth futurists wrongly claim that the decline of industrial society is *inevitable* because the earth's resources are being depleted exponentially. Against their claim, I state that natural resources will be available for the foreseeable future, that those in short supply can be replaced, and, most importantly, that technological innovation is the means by which long-range prosperity can be established. I do not claim that a golden age is inevitable, only that it is possible. Later, I will argue that predicting the social future is a far riskier business than any futurist (be he against or for growth) realizes.

4. Essential Liberalism

Four main political theories vie for human commitment: liberalism, conservatism, socialism, and communism. The division of political theories into four categories is by no means universally accepted. Communism could be subcategorized in a number of ways; some would argue that conservatism is not an authentic philosophy; liberalism might be divided into democratic liberalism and republican liberalism. It will be maintained below that although these four categories are controversial, they are not arbitrary. Moreover, a defense of liberalism will not depend on the adequacy of a particular categorical system.

These political theories are both philosophical and practical movements. Because they exist on two levels, confusion inevitably develops about them. That is why conservatives may be surprised to learn that their philosophy does not rule out socialism. On the practical level, people become communists, liberals, or conservatives because they approve particular policy recommendations of the theory to which they commit themselves. An individual may become a communist because he believes that wealth is inequitably distributed and communism calls for a redistribution of wealth. This individual may not know that Marx said that the method by which communism is to be achieved is through the establishment of a "dictatorship of the proletariat." He may not realize that this tenet of communism rules out democracy as commonly practiced. Another person may become a liberal because he approves of moral relativism—the view that each person is rationally free to adopt values for personal reasons even if those values conflict with generally accepted values—and knows that liberals seek to prevent the government from legislating morality. The same person may not realize that the liberal injunction against legislating morality raises serious doubts about whether a government is justified in passing legislation that promotes racial integration.

A difficulty that arises from the tendency if people to commit themselves to political theories because they approve of particular policy recommendations is that such people often have contradictory political goals. Another difficulty is that some adherents of a political theory try to raise their goals to the level of a philosophical theory. A liberal who observes that liberal policy abandoned the traditional *laissez-faire* attitude toward industry and called for governmental regulation of industrial practice, claims that such a policy shift was desirable because it improved the lives of most citizens. Since his conservative opponent objects to the policy shift on the grounds that it was inconsistent with traditional practice, the liberal *philosophizes* that liberalism promotes change, whereas conservatism seeks to maintain the status quo. In philosophical self-congratulation, the liberal designates his theory to be the theory of progress. Pejoratively, he calls conservatism a *reactionary* philosophy. Surprisingly, many conservatives adopt the view that they oppose change and seek to uphold tradition. Of course, they have developed their own characterizations of liberal and conservative practice. They assert that conservatives seek to preserve that which has proved viable through the crucible of experience, whereas liberals seek change for its own sake. Conservatives admit that they value order, while liberals do not, but, they add that liberals are too shortsighted to see that sweeping change often leads to chaos.

To reason in this way is not to *philosophize*, but to *rationalize*. This method of reasoning is rationalization because it proceeds in the wrong direction. It goes from practical policy recommendations to principles, whereas philosophizing proceeds from principles to practice.

Proper philosophizing requires that one develop principles for political action from conceptions of social reality. After one has demonstrated how the political principles are derived from the conceptions of social reality, then specific policy recommendations are made. This is the method of political philosophy. It was the path taken by Plato, Thomas Hobbes, Immanuel Kant, Jean-Jacques Rousseau, Adam Smith, David Ricardo, Herbert Spencer, T. H. Green, Karl Marx, Frederich Engels and others. The path of rationalization (actually pseudophilosophizing) is the road taken by liberals, conservatives, socialists, and communists whose reasoning proceeds in the wrong direction.

This book is concerned primarily with liberalism. If it is completely successful, it will be demonstrated that liberalism is a viable political philosophy, which rules out no-growth futurism. (This is a conjunction of two goals.) Liberalism is a practical, *coherent* theory which *logically* implies that the industrial way of life and economic growth should continue to be desirable goals. Liberalism is not necessarily the only political theory on which a rational, morally-justified future can be based. Nevertheless, reasons for rejecting alternative theories will be outlined. First, however, these theories must be briefly defined.

Socialism avers that all political systems must provide that a nation's major economic institutions are controlled by government. Socialism is loosely defined to include both nations in which the government *controls* major industries and nations in which the government *owns* major industries. A definition of socialism does not require that government control or own *all* industries.

Communism is alleged to be consistent with or derived from the philosophy of Karl Marx. As such it maintains that the ownership of production must be in the hands of government during the socialist stage of history and in the hands of workers during the communist stage. Communism differs from socialism in that it is a complete political theory that provides for every aspect of political (and, even, social) life.

The goal of liberalism is to provide the maximal amount of personal freedom that is consistent with the existence of an ordered, harmonious social environment. This goal is achieved through representative government, whose power to interfere with personal freedom is limited.

Conservatism originated and evolved as a reaction to liberalism.[2] Since it is necessarily "other-looking" and its champions are primarily counter-theorists, its principles are difficult to identify. Because conservatism developed gradually over a long period, its definition is vague and somewhat paradoxical. Conservatism is not defined solely in terms of its opposition to change for reasons that have been mentioned. Conservatism upholds tradition because it is believed that truths have emerged throughout the course of history.[3] Social reform is said to be unsuccessful in most cases because social planning cannot catch the complex nature of social arrangements.[4] Religious conservatives sometimes adopt the Augustinian view that human nature was corrupted by the fall of Adam and hence has to be checked by governmental authority.[5] Excessive human freedom, brought about by liberal social reform, is opposed because social reform seeks to improve imperfectible humankind and leads to chaos. A fear that conservatives always express is that of excessive freedom. Consequently, conservatives believe in legal restrictions on human freedom.[6] Thus, conservatism requires a governmentally-established social order that limits human freedom (through laws restricting alleged immoral practices, for example), permits social and political change rarely and very gradually, and, at the same time, identifies areas in which government should permit human freedom (business, for example).

These four philosophies can be integrated to some extent. For example, socialism can be joined with liberalism or conservatism. Capitalism has been espoused by liberalism and conservatism at different times. Conservatism can support monarchy as well as a republican form of government. However, conservatism is strained when it supports democracy. (That many contemporary American conservatives consider themselves to be democratic is ironic.) Liberalism, as shall be seen in more detail later, promoted republicanism initially and advanced democracy later. Liberal theory directly inspired capitalism, yet is dubious about this economic system today. Liberalism is inalterably opposed to communism and monarchical rule.

No argument will be made against socialism, but neither will this theory be defended. Socialism is neither intrinsically desirable nor fundamentally defective. Its viability depends on circumstances.

On the other hand, communism is a philosophically troubled theory whose practical expressions have run into difficulties. On the philosophical level, Marx maintained that all social institutions are determined by the economic structure of society, that certain paths of economic history are inevitable, and that a stateless society necessarily comes after the staging of a proletarian revolution.[7] (Marx's theory is more complex than this, of course, but there is no need to give a detailed account of the theory in a sketch.) There is sufficient empirical evidence to support the claim that economic systems determine all other social structures; in fact, considerable contemporary empirical evidence indicates that the social and economic structures of society are more complex than Marx thought. The introduction of the welfare state in the United States and other nations was not anticipated by Marx. Furthermore, Marx expected communism to be introduced in a highly advanced industrial society such as Great Britain or Germany.[8] Finally, the experience of Russia shows that the events that were to have inevitably followed the revolution have not occurred.

One must be careful when passing from the *theory* of Marxism to its *practice*. It is believed by many observers of communist nations that deviations from the theory are the rule. Marx claimed that the revolution was inevitable and would follow a predictable pattern. In other words, the communist revolution would have occurred whether or not Marx had written about it. If these observers of communist practice are correct, then the Marxian theory is defective for its predictions have not been realized.

Before I proceed, I want to make clear that I use the expression "communist nations" to refer to those political states that claim to follow Marxist theory. I do not contend that these nations interpret Marx in the same way. They are united in the sense that they are not liberal in form and oppose liberal policies to various degrees.

Despite these criticisms, it might be argued that it would be worthwhile to revise Marxian theory since it seeks to protect those who are economically and politically oppressed. One factor alone would stand in the way of making this attempt. A Marxian type of revolution justifies dictatorial government which promotes tyranny. Marx did not realize the extent to which people *naturally* tend to oppress others. This behavior does not emanate from the human desire for economic security as Marx maintained; it is an ubiquitous human tendency that can be avoided only by the institution of rules limiting the power of government. More will be said about the tendency of human beings to be authoritarian when liberalism is discussed.

Unlike liberalism and communism, conservatism does not possess a coherent set of axioms on which its practical policies are based. It is, and has been, a *reaction* to liberalism. Before liberalism existed, there was no coherent political theory because political authority was wielded by those who possessed the greatest power. These people claimed to be placed in power by God, but they did not talk about a divinely directed method of legitimately *obtaining* power. Conservatism, inevitably, has been espoused by an entrenched class—sometimes economic, sometimes military, and occasionally religious—which has sought to retain its advantages. When conservatism defended the Roman Catholic Church, it was dogmatic. When it defended monarchy, it was authoritarian. In either of these guises, conservatives sought to limit personal freedom. Today, the entrenched class is capitalistic, and thus conservatives argue against authority that might restrict business and proclaim the virtues of personal freedom, which permits industrialists and entrepreneurs to act unrestrainedly. Philosophically, one of the greatest defects in conservatism is that it cannot provide rules that guide people in making changes. All conservatives recognize that some social and economic changes are salubrious in principle. If they did not, they would be hopelessly reactionary. Nonetheless, conservatives do not develop rules to determine what kind of changes are desirable and what kind are not. If they approve of changes, they do so after the fact. Contemporary conservatives approve of a free market, but they did not given their approval until it had become a reality. In the United States, conservatives were the isolationists of the 1920s and 1930s. They now champion American intervention in European, Asian, and African affairs. Without principles for guiding change, conservatism seems to invite ad hoc measures.

In discussing liberalism, I will trace the historical development of the classical theory and its contemporary version. It is my conviction that studying the historical development of a political theory is an extremely useful way of separating the essential and the accidental aspects of the theory. One group of critics claims that liberalism is an obsolete theory (communists, new leftists, and others) and another group claims that its practical form contradicts its philosophical principles (Robert Paul Wolff, among others). A historical description will reveal that there are certain fundamental principles that remain unchanged in liberal theory and that nonfundamental principles have changed as beliefs have evolved and as social conditions have changed. After the classical and contemporary forms of liberalism are presented, as essential liberalism will be developed. The essential features of liberalism have been present throughout liberal history, although they have not always dominated practical politics.

The History of English Liberalism

Liberalism was introduced by John Locke in the late seventeenth century and was amplified by other British philosophers, such as John Stuart Mill, Herbert Spencer, and T. H. Green. Economic theorists, Adam Smith and J. M. Keynes, for example, eventually espoused this theory. Liberalism influenced philosophers and political thinkers of other nations. Rousseau, Voltaire, Montesquieu, Toqueville, von Humboldt, and even the great Kant are only a few. Liberalism was the philosophy of the American and French revolutions. It was the personal theory of Thomas Jefferson and Thomas Paine. Together the Declaration of Independence and the Constitution can be read as practical expressions of liberal philosophy. Liberalism is the source of the famed Declaration of the Rights of Man and Citizen, which was adopted by the French revolutionaries. This document was derived from the English Declaration of Rights and the American Declaration of Independence. The French statement served as a model for the Declaration of Human Rights adopted by the United Nations in 1948. The evidence is clear. Liberal philosophy has been the most important force in the shaping of modern Western political systems.

The influence of liberalism has been so great that its most vigorous, ideological competitor, communism, is a reaction to liberalism. Many commentators are aware that Marx took basic concepts of economic theory from Smith.[9] But they often overlook the fact that Marx's opposition to capitalism and liberal democracy sprang from his belief that these forms could not achieve the moral goals for which they were instituted. Marx's moral criticism of liberal government and economics was based on an acceptance of the ultimate liberal goal—the attainment of universal liberty for all individuals.[10]

Liberalism evolved unconsciously from the interaction of barons and kings in England between the thirteenth and seventeenth centuries. The *Magna Carta* (the Great Charter) is generally thought to have been the embryonic expression of liberalism because it introduced the notion of "due process" into English law.[11] Under feudalism, the myth arose that the king owned all the land. The king parceled it out to local lords (barons) who in turn let it out to vassels. The vassels owed service and money to the barons and the barons were similarly obligated to the king. The baron guaranteed the peace of the community and ensured judicial fairness when disputes arose among subjects. King John, after an unsuccessful war with France, sought to increase the services and money extracted from the barons. They resisted and captured the town of London. The Great Charter was drawn and submitted to the king, who initially refused to sign it. However, since John did not have the means to resist, he finally agreed to accept the charter, and it was promulgated on June 19, 1215. It contained many provisions, but the most important ones limited the power of the king. The jurisdiction of the feudal courts (Article 34) and baronial privileges were ensured. Free elections were guaranteed to the Church (Article 1). Free commerce was protected by the guarantee of the liberties to London and other cities (Article 13). Most importantly, Article 39 has been interpreted as guaranteeing due process.

No freeman shall be taken and imprisoned or dis-seized, exiled or in any way destroyed, nor shall we go upon him nor send upon him, except by the lawful judgment of one's peers and by the law of the land.

The importance of the Magna Carta is that it established the principle that the king was subject to written law and that persons accused of a crime could not be denied life, liberty, or property without judgment of their peers. The document was confirmed by Parliament in the reign of Henry III, John's son. In 1297, Parliament issued a modified form of the charter, which now serves as its standard form.

The next important step in the development of liberal theory took place after the death of Elizabeth I. She, along with her father and grandfather, had increased the political and economic power of the nation by establishing a strong centralized government. When James I succeeded her, Parliament sought to reestablish its power. Parliament had been called into session more often by the Tudors than by previous rulers. In order to establish his authority against the Roman Catholic Church and to obtain money to support his extravagances, Henry VIII had convened Parliament and, basically, obtained what he wanted from it. Elizabeth I, being a shrewd politician, had used subtle means to achieve her ends and created no breach with Parliament. The story of James I was quite different. He vigorously proclaimed the "divine right of kings" at a time when Parliament was feeling its importance. Certain groups in Parliament and the judiciary invoked a social contract theory which stated that the king held power on the condition that he ruled wisely, fairly, and effectively. If these conditions were unfulfilled, the king could be considered to have abdicated his position and his subjects would have the right to set up a new government. Sir Edward Coke, a chief justice of the Court of Common Pleas and later a chief justice of the King's Bench, issued a number of rulings which asserted that the will of kings and Parliament were subordinate to the fundamental law of the land, which was expressed in common law principles.[12]

Coke also interpreted the Magna Carta as ensuring *due process* to all free men, not only to barons. Subsequent generations of scholars have expressed doubt that Coke interpreted the charter correctly. Nevertheless, Coke's interpretation has eventually become standard.

When Charles I ascended the throne, succeeding his father James I, the dispute between the royal seat and Parliament dragged on. The first eruption of conflict took place in 1628 when Charles I called Parliament into session to obtain money needed to pay for unsuccessful wars waged with France. Parliament generously supplied the money in return for the king's acceptance of the Petition of Right, the second of three documents that form the basis of the English theory of liberal government. The petition stated that (1) taxation required the consent of Parliament, (2) a subject could not be imprisoned without definite cause being shown, to which the accused had the right to answer according to law, (3) troops could not be billeted on the people without their consent, and (4) martial law could not be imposed on civilians in peacetime.[13]

These rights did not immediately change the course of government. Another Parliament was convened in 1629, but Charles I dissolved it and ruled for eleven years with complete disregard for the Petition of Right. He recalled Parliament in 1640, again to obtain money. This proved to be his undoing. Constant conflict raged until Parliament, under the leadership of Oliver Cromwell, beheaded Charles in 1649. Cromwell ruled as protector from 1653 to 1658. His position was indistinguishable from that of a king. He was so authoritarian that Charles II, the son of Charles I, was brought back to rule England when Richard Cromwell failed to assume authority after his father's death.

The Restoration (of monarchy) was an attempt to divide political authority between the king and Parliament. Initially, Charles II was content with this arrangement. Conflict developed over the issue of succession. The king wanted the Roman Catholic Duke of York to succeed him rather than his Protestant daughter Mary. Since most Englishmen were Protestant by then, they were opposed to Charles's choice. Despite public clamor, the Duke of York ascended the throne and assumed the name James II. As Parliament feared, he attempted to restore Roman Catholicism, and as a result Parliament deposed him.

Parliament was called into session to set up a new government. A dispute arose among Tories (conservatives) and Whigs (liberals). The Tories wanted Mary to ascend the throne because this would uphold the monarchical tradition. The Whigs wanted the throne to be offered jointly to Mary and her husband William because this would demonstrate that the normal means of succession had been abandoned. They reasoned that, since James II had broken the so-called social contract between the people and himself, he had in effect abdicated the throne and Parliament could renegotiate a contract with anyone. As we know, the Whigs attained their desire.

Before William and Mary ascended the throne, they were forced to accept the Declaration of Rights, which when passed by Parliament in 1689 became the Bill of Rights.[14] This was the third document of English liberal theory. It ensured freedom of speech, frequent parliamentary sessions, and the control of taxation by Parliament. Subjects were given the right to petition the crown, and juries were to be selected fairly. Cruel punishment and unusual fines, excessive bail, and the power of the king to avoid enforcing laws were forbidden. Finally, the king was prohibited from maintaining a standing army in peacetime without the consent of Parliament.

Subsequent acts reinforced the gains established by the Bill of Rights. In 1694, a Triennial Act was passed providing for elections every three years.[15] The Treason Act of 1696 protected opponents of the king by requiring that anyone accused of treason be allowed to have legal counsel and see an indictment before a trial could ensure.[16] The Act of Settlement of 1701 revoked the prinicple that judges sat solely at the pleasure of the king. Thereafter, judges would hold office for life unless charges of misconduct were proved in Parliament.[17]

The Philosophical Development of English Liberalism

The development of liberalism was influenced by the interests of a variety of groups. As disputes continued, ideals emerged, first as rationalizations of those who wanted to acquire political power or achieve personal gains, but eventually as principles in which people believed. First, *procedural* rights were won. Life, liberty, and property could not be taken away by the government unless certain rules were followed. These procedures established a legal concept of personal freedom. To be sure, the legal assertion of the right of personal freedom was made on behalf of property holders. Nevertheless, the *principle* of personal freedom was engendered by the arguments of lords who sought to limit the power of monarchs. However, substantive rights were not granted. For example, lords were not given, nor did they seek, an *equitable* distribution of property. That is, there was no attempt to distribute the goods of the land according to moral principles.

Second, the king and Parliament were limited by a system of common law. Initially, war between the king and Parliament was fought over who had the right to rule by will. Each desired absolute freedom to direct the activities of the nation. Eventually, the courts asserted that the actions of both should be governed by principles in which the interests of *all* citizens were taken into account. The basis of the courts' ruling was that legal power ultimately rested with the people but that people gave up some of their autonomy to the government on the condition that the government would maintain and settle their disagreements. This is the social contract theory. It was introduced in ancient times but was later reformulated by British philosophers, such as Thomas Hooker and John Locke, who sought to cast the English system of government into a rational framework. Parliament adopted the theory and interpreted itself to be the representative of the citizenry.

Third, the notion of representative government evolved. The idea that people could be represented by a few men of a special class originated in Ancient Greece. It was recognized early in English history. It took a long time, however, for Englishmen to recognize that people needed the right to vote regularly in order to check the power of their representatives. The suffrage movement, which gradually extended the vote to all men and eventually to women, began in this period. It did not gain momentum until the nineteenth century and only fulfilled its purpose in the twentieth.

Fourth, the right of revolution was recognized. It was reasoned that the purpose of government is to create a social environment that satisfies people's interests. If government does not achieve this goal, it has not performed its contractual obligations and hence is at war with the people. Therefore, the people can rightfully establish a new government.

These various beliefs were synthesized into a political philosophy by

John Locke in his *Second Treatise of Government*.[18] It is generally argued that the second treatise was written in 1689 after the revolution of 1688. Recently, Peter Laslett maintained with some cogency that the second treatise was written earlier, somewhere between 1679 and 1681.[19] The significance of this dispute is that the earlier date would establish that Locke's work was original, whereas the later date suggests that Locke merely rationalized the revolution. On either account, Locke's thesis is a coherent, liberal defense of representative government.

Locke used the notions of natural law and natural rights. He argued that in a state of nature, before governments are established, people live in perfect freedom to act as they see fit. In this state, people are equal, but their actions are limited by the laws of nature. (In this respect, he disagreed with Thomas Hobbes, who maintained that people are at war with each other in presociety.) People are bound to preserve peace, sustain humankind, and refrain from injuring others. If a person violates these rules, he is at war with others and is subject to punishment. Because many people tend to violate the rights of others, Locke theorized that peace and harmony can be maintained successfully only by the establishment of a civil government. Accordingly, a government is formed whose purpose is to preserve the natural rights of life, liberty, and property which are shared by all people.

Locke defined property as land that people have appropriated by their own labor. God has given the earth and its resources to everyone, but people remove land from general ownership through labor. Governments are instituted primarily to preserve this property right and to make laws governing the use, distribution, and transfer of property. Rather strangely, Locke maintained that the primary reason that anyone threatens another's life or freedom is to obtain the other's property. Thus, the defense of property is said to be the practical purpose of the state.

A proper government, according to Locke, is one that divides the power of the state. Specifically, Locke desired to separate the legislative body from the executive and federative (treaty-making) body. Sovereignty ultimately rests with the people, and Locke argued that the legislature ought to be elected by the people. The executive is entrusted with carrying out the law. If he exceeds his authority, he can be deposed. If the legislature goes beyond its duties, it can be dissolved and a new government established. In order to avoid the latter abuse of authority, Locke called for the regular election of the legislature.

Locke's government was representative. In practice, England did not become democratic until the late nineteenth century. It took so long to realize democracy because Parliament was controlled by large property owners who sought to reserve legislative membership for themselves. The inflated importance that Locke gave to property contributed to this condition.

What we must note is that liberal theory was grounded in the desire to promote personal freedom and to prevent government from restricting that freedom. When governments infringed on a person's freedom, they were condemned as tyrannies.

Many of Locke's claims were disputed and his arguments rejected for their superficiality. Subsequent liberal political philosophers have denied the reality of a state of nature, the reasonableness of natural law or natural rights, and the actual existence of a social contract. The conception of property and the priority given to it have been rejected by most liberals. Nevertheless, Lockean beliefs are retained by liberals: the priority given to personal liberty, the need to limit governmental authority (tyranny), and the utility of representative government.

Almost two hundred years after Locke wrote this second treatise, the idea of personal freedom was developed eloquently by John Stuart Mill. He articulated the notion that government governs best when it governs least. In his famous essay *On Liberty*,[20] Mill argued that government can limit the freedom of its citizens only for the sake of their protection. He firmly denied that government has the right to restrict the liberty of citizens for their own good.

By the time Mill wrote *On Liberty*, the right of religious freedom was fully developed. Political theorists were aware that religious zealots tried to force dissenters to follow their beliefs. Religious persecution within states and religious wars among states had been common since the time of Martin Luther. Liberals opposed religious intolerance, not only because religious conflicts destroyed social stability, but because there was no way to establish which religious or moral claims were true. As Mill argued, all (intelligent and educated) people recognize their own fallibility in principle but few *act* as though their opinions might be mistaken. To force others to agree with one's concepts of religion, morality, or even human welfare is to act as if one were infallible. Mill concluded that any action which tends to restrict personal freedom in these matters is tyranny.

When Locke wrote, property was thought to be land because those who were seated in the House of Lords were the landed gentry. A century later, the Industrial Revolution was well underway in England and a redefinition of property was introduced by Adam Smith.[21] In Smith, we recognize the founder of the theory of classical economics. Since labor was turning more toward industry than agriculture, the real wealth of nations was in the hands of merchants and entrepreneurs. Capital, both money and machinery, was defined as property and people were said to be free to use it as they saw fit. It was argued that the tyrannical tendencies of government would most likely be manifest in the appropriation of capital from merchants and entrepreneurs. In order to promote free enterprise and to resist government tyranny, Smith endorsed the doctrine of the Physiocrats: *Laissez faire et laissez passer, le monde va de lui-même* ("Do not interfere, the world will take care of itself"). In essence, Smith applied the liberal theory to an evolving industrial environment.

Although there were other contributors to classical liberalism, Locke, Smith, and Mill were the founders of the movement. As can be noted, the theory did not develop at once. In fact, even though Locke initiated the theory and put most of its pieces in place, the term "liberal" was not used until the early nineteenth century. The term "liberales" was originally used by Spaniards to refer to followers of Locke and was imported to England by Tories. These conservative politicians used it as a pejorative name for their Whig opponents, implying by the term that the Whigs were importing foreign ideas and concepts. Eventually, Whigs adopted the term and gave it its contemporary meaning.[22]

The Evolution of Contemporary Liberalism

Classical liberalism, as a philosophical thesis and as a political movement, underwent alterations as it met counterarguments and the realities of political practice.

The aforementioned denial of the existence of natural law and natural rights undercuts the liberal theoretical foundation. Liberals responded to these philosophical maneuvers by basing liberal government on a utilitarian theory of morality, according to which human happiness—the goal of utilitarian morality—could be attained in a political society in which human freedom was ensured.

The most significant changes in liberalism occurred as a consequence of its practical application in the form of liberal government. The main casualty of the clash between theory and practice was the notion of negative or laissez-faire government.

Classical liberals believed that business uncontaminated by governmental restriction, or free enterprise, would increase individual liberty. Smith realized that this goal could be achieved only if competition were open. But in fact, unrestrained business activity led to the development of monopolies which produced a "closed" marketplace.

The liberal response to this turn of events was to call for government curbs on business activities in order to protect the consumer and the worker. In other words, liberals replaced negative government with active government. Since big businessmen had formed an entrenched class, it was only natural that their philosophy became the new conservataism. Thus, since the early twentieth century, conservatives have espoused the classical liberal line; that is, they have argued that government intervention in business is tyranny and a denial of human freedom. In the last twenty years of this century, the person who has most closely perorated classical liberal jargon is President Ronald Reagan—the Republican conservative. Why conservatism took this path is a story for another book.

The fact that practical political philosophy was turned upside down led many critics of liberalism, Robert Paul Wolff, for example,[23] to claim that liberal philosophy was dead. It seemed that advocating government intervention after championing laissez-faire government required fundamental changes in theory. Other legislation that has been endorsed by contemporary liberal politicians—social security, minimum wage, regulation of business practices, governmental health insurance, socialized medicine in Great Britain, affirmative action programs in the United States, and so on—*suggests* that contemporary liberals retain the name without the substance. It is argued that only vestiges remain of the liberal fear of government tyranny and the desire for personal autonomy. It is also argued that one of classical liberalism's most important assertions—that government officials abuse their power when they actively promote their personal conception of the moral and social good—has been discarded. No one has expressed opposition to this practice more eloquently than John Stuart Mill in *On Liberty*.

> The object of this Essay is to assert one very simple principle, as entitled to govern absolutely the dealings of society and the individual in the way of compulsion and control, whether the means used by physical force in the form of legal penalties, or the moral coercion of public opinion. That principle is, that the sole end for which mankind is warranted, individually or collectively, in interfering with the liberty of action of any of their number, is self-protection. That the only purpose for which power can be rightfully exercised over any member of a civilized community, against his will, is to prevent harm to others. His own good, either physical or moral, is not a sufficient warrant. He cannot rightfully be compelled to do or forbear because it will be better for him to do so, because it will make him happier, because, in the opinion of others, to do so would be wise, or even right. . . . The only part of the conduct of any one, for which he is amenable to

society, is that which concerns others. In the part which merely concerns himself, his independence is, of right, absolute. Over himself, over his own body and mind, the individual is sovereign.[24]

There is no question that contemporary liberal practice is out of tune with the sentiments expressed by Mill in this famous quotation. However, contemporary liberal philosophers, such as Robert Dahl, state that changing conditions have justified changes in liberal practice. Whereas kings once had excessive power to dominate people's lives, industry, through its influence on legislatures, has developed excessive power which has had to be checked. Furthermore, the freedom of enterprise supported by liberals such as Smith and Mill was the freedom of small business—business that could justifiably be called *private* enterprise. Small business could be said to be an expression of the individual's attempt to obtain happiness. As Robert Dahl has argued, the development of giant stockholding companies has made big business *public* enterprise and, hence, the proper subject of government control.[25]

The point of Dahl's reply to the Wolff-like criticism is that the *ends* of liberalism have not changed; only the *means* to liberal ends have been altered. Contemporary liberals still seek to promote individual freedom and to limit tyranny. Before, the threat of tyranny was from government, and the source of freedom was private enterprise; but in contemporary times, the threat of oppression is from monopolistic business, and government is the only force strong enough to control it. The liberal shift toward controlling industry led to most of the labor reforms and industrial restrictions that had been instituted by the last half of the twentieth century.

A second major shift in liberal practice is the increasing role of government in promoting civil rights. Classical liberals thought that people would develop intellectually, morally, and emotionally if their behavior were not inhibited by government fiat. Consequently, the liberty sought by liberals was freedom from institutional restraint. This freedom is fundamentally procedural. For example, the civil rights of blacks were ensured according to classical liberal principles, when the Fourteenth Amendment was passed *and* when local government rules limiting the participation of blacks in public contexts (segregation in schools, restaurants, and business establishments; poll taxes; voting requirements which were intended to disqualify blacks; discrimination in hiring and housing; and so on) were declared unconstitutional or were federally restrained. These steps were taken to guarantee that blacks would be granted *in practice* the same freedom as whites. On the other hand, the government has set up affirmative action programs that force whites to accept blacks (and other minorities) in a variety of contexts and that force blacks to follow institutionally prescribed paths of social advancement. To classical liberals such policies are tyrannical because they force people to follow the moral and social paths that the government considers desirable.

Contemporary liberals justify this change in policy on the grounds that some classical liberal beliefs had to be altered as a consequence of developments in psychological theory. Once again, it is argued that the fundamental goals of liberalism have not changed; only the means to liberal ends have changed. Contemporary liberals deny that human beings are capable of achieving complete self-development simply by being freed from institutional harassment. The classical liberal belief in absolute self-determination is based on the view that people are psychologically the same regardless of the social context. Hobbes and Locke expressed this view when they theorized that people in presociety were capable of rationally recognizing the deficiencies of nonpolitical existence and calculating how a social contract could overcome their difficulties. In another context, Adam Smith maintained that every consumer, regardless of his education and training, is capable of determining which product he needs, which products are well-made, and so on. According to contemporary psychological theory, the social context in which a person matures determines to a great extent what he desires and what he is capable of doing. For a person to develop fully, he must grow up in a social environment that encourages him to develop his abilities and to set high goals. Because of this shift in psychological theory, then, it is argued that the government must ensure that citizens are given the opportunity to maximize self-development. This, at any rate, is the justification for positive governmental action in social matters.

Essential Liberalism

It will be argued that the main shifts in liberal policy are justified by fundamental liberal principles. Conditions (the status of business) and beliefs (regarding the psychology of the individual) have changed and this has required changes in means. These changes have been consistent with liberal principles.

This does not mean that every liberal proposal to limit industry or every affirmative action program should be endorsed. Liberalism cannot tolerate an infinite number of changes in policy even if the changes are introduced to advance liberty. Liberalism must have some unchangeable tenets or it is not a distinctive theory. At this point, then, it is necessary to indicate that which is unique about liberalism and to point out the policy limitations beyond which liberals cannot go. An essential liberalism will be developed which will identify ends and some necessary means to those ends that are unchangeable. If the ends are no longer thought to be morally desirable or if the means are not feasible, then liberalism will have been falsified.

The fundamental beliefs about human nature that are vital to liberal philosophy are that (1) people are fundamentally self-interested, (2) self-interest points toward happiness, and (3) people, because of biological and social variability, are temperamentally diverse and consequently seek happiness in different ways. Liberals have disagreed as to the nature of happiness. Some have defined it hedonistically (i.e., in terms of pleasure), others have defined it as an intellectual or spiritual state, and still others have put forth purely egoistic principles (Hobbes). From the standpoint of political theory, these differences do not matter. What is important is that human beings are thought of as being *individualistic*, as having personal goals that deserve to be satisfied. Furthermore, the desires of human beings must be satisfied in a variety of ways. As John Stuart Mill expressed it, people require eccentric self-development.[26] The aforementioned conception of human nature led to the moral concept of *human rights* and the legal concept of *civil rights*.

Two necessary *means* of achieving self-development are thought to be (1) *freedom*, so that people can pursue their individual paths, and (2) *material well-being*, which is said to be necessary for happiness. In regard to this latter point, some people identify happiness with material well-being; most do not. For those who see higher human ends, material well-being is considered to be a minimal condition of developing higher goals. This is not surprising when we consider that liberalism was initially inspired by the attempt of English landowners to protect their property from appropriation by kings. Locke's reduction of civil rights to property rights and Smith's avowal of capitalism demonstrate the centrality of material well-being in liberal thought. Nor has this situation changed in contemporary times. The black civil rights movement, when it was directed by liberals, used economic differences between whites and blacks as the barometer by which to measure the success of the movement.[27] The women's liberation movement, most recently, has sought to attain economic equality with men above all other goals.[28]

According to classical liberal philosophers, society is joined for cooperation; government is formed to protect people from aggression. Liberals have disagreed as to how political society came into being, but again, this does not matter. The important feature of liberal theory, which has outlived classical liberalism, is that political society serves human beings and is *judged* by the effectiveness with which it performs its function.

A fact of social life, according to liberals, is that people form subgroups in order to achieve common goals. In the political sphere, these subgroups are called factions. They seek to translate their will into law, to crush opposition, and to impose their vision of the good life and their social priorities on all people. This characteristic of factions emanates from "self-interested" human nature. If a faction is successful, it will control the administration of law. People who are uncommitted to a faction or who belong to a politically ineffective one are tyrannized. The inevitability of factional selfishness is stated with admirable bluntness by James Madison in the *Federalist Papers.*[29]

From the liberal notion of factionalism, a central belief emerged: that government and factions tend to be tyrannical and must be controlled so that the self-interests of people are served. This belief led to constitutional restrictions on government power, minimal rights being granted to individuals, and representative government. This last feature was introduced to ensure that *all* factions, even small ones, are served by government.

In summary, according to the liberal theory, *the goal of political life is the creation and maintenance of a social environment that accommodates eccentric personal development and limits the tyrannical tendency of factions.*

The liberals infer two political purposes from their conception of social reality: (1) the molding of a political system that maximizes opportunities for eccentric self-development and (2) incorporating within the political structures safeguards against tyranny. Therefore, *essential liberalism is the belief that people ought to operate in a social and political environment that permits maximal personal freedom and limits tyranny.*

This definition must be qualified because it is necessary to limit personal freedom in order that conflicts between people are minimized and to ensure the efficient attainment of shared social goals. Therefore, "maximal personal freedom" can be defined as *the greatest amount of opportunity for self-development in light of the limitations necessary to establish an effective social system.* The qualifier on personal freedom does not permit the imposition of extreme restrictions on personal freedom in the name of social harmony and order. If this were allowed, the distinction between liberalism and conservatism would be erased, or liberal goals would be reduced to verbal niceties. In order to avoid these consequences, conceptions of minimal personal freedom were introduced in documents like the American Bill of Rights, the French Declaration of the Rights of Man and Citizen, and the United Nations Universal Declaration of the Rights of Man. The provisions in these documents are so well-known that there is no need to state them.

In summary, liberals believe that the necessary means by which maximal personal freedom is ensured and the tyrannical tendencies of factions are avoided are through (1) the legal promulgation of human rights (civil rights), (2) the institution of representative government, and (3) the legal restrictions of the powers of government.

Certainly, all those who call themselves liberals do not subscribe to essential liberalism. Essential liberalism is an attempt to render liberal theory coherent and to make sense of much of liberal policy history. Furthermore, it gives us a standard for distinguishing between good and bad liberal practice.

With regard to the latter point, policy recommendations that are inconsistent with liberal theory are often overwhelmingly supported by liberals and enacted into law. It is probably true that liberals, being carried away by their desire to satisfy *individual* interests (a liberal goal), have promoted laws that give so much power to government that it approaches tyranny (a nonliberal means). Two tendencies should be avoided. First, liberals should not redefine their theory to accommodate such policy changes because this deprives liberalism of genuine substantive content. Second, liberals should *not* abandon their philosophy sumply because some liberals misunderstand the basic theory. Rather, liberals who are aware of the deviant nature of some practical recommendations should voice their objections and wait until the time is ripe to redirect social and political action.

Falsifying Conditions of Liberalism

This discussion of falsifying conditions is limited to those that are unique to liberalism. General problems related to moral and political theories are not considered. For example, all cognitive moral theories (such as utilitarianism) face the problem of demonstrating how moral knowledge is acquired. All political systems that are justified on moral grounds (as liberalism is) must rationally demonstrate that (1) morality has political ramifications and (2) a particular system fulfills moral needs. These problems will not be considered on the *pragmatic* ground that we must confront only those problems that are raised by the opposition. Most critics of liberalism do not pose fundamental philosophical questions; they assume a connection between morality and political systems. A moral and political anarchist would probably raise fundamental philosophical questions, but such individuals are rare and do not usually form moral and political action groups. Political and moral anarchists should be addressed in a separate work.

The criticisms of liberalism are generally of two kinds: those that question the basic goals of liberalism and those that suggest that the means to liberal ends are defective in some way. Four falsifying conditions will be discussed. The first two are relevant to the desirability of liberal goals; the fourth to the effectiveness of liberal means; and the third to both. Liberalism would be falsified if one or more of the following claims were shown to be true.

1. The liberal concept of individualism is empirically false. That is people are not temperamentally different, self-interested, and/or seekers of happiness. If the liberal concept of individualism were falsified, then there would be no need to promote personal liberty.

2. Government is not morally obligated to provide a social environment that accommodates individualism. This claim would be verified if government (a) could satisfy with moral impunity the interests of special groups or (b) were driven by God or natural laws to direct human beings toward certain specifiable ends.

3. Political leaders are infallible and morally incorruptible. If this claim were true, then there would be no need to provide individual freedom since wise, just rulers would pass and implement laws that direct people according to their genuine interests and needs.

4. The traditional means of liberalism—representative government, civil rights, and limitations on political authority—are easily subverted and other political means provide greater assurance that individual interests could be satisfied.

Let us consider the first two falsifying conditions. By rejecting the concept of individualism, we are forced to deny the teachings of psychology and sociology of the past one hundred years. Cultural and personal relativity—the belief that people are temperamentally different—are cornerstones of these social sciences. (This does not imply that ethical relativity, which is a normative theory, is true.) To reject the belief that governments are not morally obligated to provide an environment which promotes individualism, we must revive such concepts as natural law or the divine right of kings. Not that some philosophers do not try to do this. However, since such attempts run counter to the mainstream of contemporary thought, it is unnecessary to consider them in a practical context. Admittedly some nations still operate as if there were a divine right of political rulers, but current "divine right of king" movements are atavistic since they merely reiterate the arguments made by previous rulers (James I of England, Phillip II of Spain).

There seems to be a greater tendency of people to take seriously the third falsifying condition of liberalism, that is, people often think that political leaders might be found who, through intellectual and/or moral superiority, could direct people against their wills for their own good. Although other people doubt that political leaders who are infallible or morally incorruptible could exist in reality, they still *act* as though they could. History shows, however, that most political leaders do not retain their intellectual ability or their altruism when they are given absolute authority. They are corrupted. There simply are many more Caligula-types than there are Marcus Aurelius-types. Nor can one judge that he has met one of the latter by reading campaign promises. The counter-argument to the third falsifying condition of liberalism is that government should be organized according to the probable behavior of political leaders, not their *possible* behavior. Leaders may be intellectually and morally superior throughout their term of office, but they most likely will not be. Therefore, it is preferable to base political institutions on the latter probability.

Many people have argued that the fourth falsifying condition has been met. They have said that representative government, civil rights, and limitations on political authority are not sufficient to deal with the problems of a complicated social system. Two factors mitigate against the success of the traditional liberal system. First, change takes place too slowly in a liberal government to meet the needs of the people. Second, entrenched interests control the government.

This potentially falsifying condition requires more serious consideration than the others because it was widely circulated in the United States in the 1960s. Numerous people, including many former liberals, believed it to be true. In fact, its wide acceptance hastened the decline in the popularity of liberalism. Before 1960, most Americans who did not claim to be moderates (the most popular political stance in the United States in recent years) claimed to be liberals. Now, many more Americans say that they are conservatives. Few liberals today admit their allegiance unhesitatingly or unreservedly. It is not that this falsifying condition has stronger evidence or better logic behind it. It is only that it is believed.

The claim that liberal government acts too slowly to satisfy the needs of people is allegedly exemplified by the failure of the black civil rights movement of the 1960s to attain all its goals. That entrenched classes control the government is supposedly exemplified by American foreign policy since World War II.

The black movement was a case of seeking to maximize individual rights for a deprived minority. The moral goal of the movement was to create a social environment that provided opportunity for the personal self-development of blacks. The legal goal was to extend civil rights to a class of people who were previously denied them. Hereafter, to take into account the eventual scope of the movement, it will be referred to as the civil rights movement.

The civil rights movement began at the end of World War II and accelerated after the Supreme Court declared in 1954 that segregated education was unconstitutional. This movement initially sought to provide both procedural equality before the law as required by classical liberalism and social opportunity as required by contemporary liberalism. The former was attained; inroads were made on the latter. In general, the movement sought legal and social opportunities for minorities.

Through the years, bigoted whites continued to find ways to segregate themselves from blacks and other minorities and to maintain economic advantages for members of their own race. By the mid-1960s, a truly racially integrated society had not been achieved, nor had incomes of minorities reached the levels attained by whites. This led to the rejection of liberalism by minorities and many white sympathizers.

There are two reasons for thinking that the claim that liberalism failed in this case is mistaken. First, being founded on the belief that human beings are selfish and imperfect, liberalism did not contend that an ideal society, that is, a society in which the interests of all people would be satisfied, can be developed. (Marx promised this, not liberals.) It assumes that people naturally create factions. Thus, the white counterattacks were as predictable as the evolution of black and minority power. What one would expect to emerge, if liberalism were successful, would be a "balance of power." And, in fact, something like this evolved. Minorities made some political and economic advances. To be sure, minorities did not obtain all that they were morally entitled to, but they made definite inroads. They obtained almost all of their procedural rights and extended their social opportunities.

Second, liberalism was judged by a false standard. The goal of the civil rights movement subtly shifted from the attainment of institutional equality (which provides greater social, economic, and political *opportunity*) to the realization of social, political, and economic *equality*. It is for *not* having provided social, political, and economic equality for minorities that liberalism is said to have failed. This is a false standard by which to judge liberalism because liberalism promises to provide the personal freedom to attain equality, but leaves the outcome to human ingenuity. Liberalism cannot be judged to be at fault for not guaranteeing the end result of social and political action when it seeks to provide only the *means* for self-development.

Furthermore, the refusal of liberalism to ensure the end result of a political and social process is well-founded. As stated earlier, liberalism is based on the recognition of human fallibility and the oppressiveness of extreme political power. To ensure the outcome of the civil rights movement is to treat the opinions of civil rights advocates as if they were incontrovertibly true and to deny freedom to those who contest these opinions.

In conclusion on this point, the most significant *institutional* barriers to minority advances have been removed: minority members can and do run for political office, legal institutions hear the complaints of minority members who allege that they have been denied access to white neighborhoods, open-enrollment policies have been implemented in primary and secondary schools (although forced integration of schools has not succeeded), affirmative action programs favor the admission of minority candidates to colleges and professional schools, and business opportunities for minorities have increased. By removing institutional barriers and providing social opportunity through affirmative action, liberalism has been vindicated, not discredited. The rest is up to people.

That military factions in this country have persuaded the government to pursue aggressive policies toward such nations as Vietnam and industry has used its influence to obtain favorable legislation supposedly demonstrate that entrenched classes control government. These cases will not be examined in detail because many of the points made in the civil rights discussion are relevant here. For example, critics of liberal government fail to realize that liberals expect people and groups to act factiously. Therefore, there is nothing surprising about the actions of the military and industry. Again, the goal of liberalism is to establish a "balance of power." Moreover, the critics of liberalism formed counterfactions that significantly modified United States policy regarding Vietnam and business. The war in Vietnam was ended and American foreign policy did not assume an aggressive stance until the taking of American hostages in Iran in late 1979. In effect, American antiliberal critics of foreign policy unintentionally verified the liberal theory by forming counterfactions which limited the power of the military. The same antiliberals modified the influence of industry on government and obtained pollution restrictions on industrial practice and development.

In general, those who have maintained that liberalism is obsolete were unaware of, or ignored, the liberal opposition to assumptions of infallibility. These critics were so confident in their own infallibility and virtue, that they boldly sought to translate their will into law. Anything short of total victory was considered defeat. Compromise was out of the question. On the other hand, philosophical liberals, who are fully aware of their own fallibility and who respect individualism and freedom, invariably seek compromise.

The point is that many critics of liberalism argue that liberalism failed by the mid-1960s because they are unaware of basic liberal tenets. In other words, their commitment to liberalism is based on their commitment to particular liberal policies (for example, advancement of the civil rights of minorities and opposition to industrial exploitation of labor) and not on an awareness of the philosophical foundations of liberalism.

Having made this criticism of liberal critics, I would like to close with a quotation from a minority report of a Supreme Court decision by Oliver Wendell Holmes. This statement was made in order to defend freedom of speech, but it also can be generalized to support intellectual tolerance and humility. For sheer eloquence, it may not be matched in the canons of liberal literature.

Persecution for the expression of opinions seems to be perfectly logical. If you have no doubt of your premises or your power and want a certain result with all your heart you naturally express your wishes in law and sweep away all opposition. To allow opposition by speech seems to indicate that you think the speech impotent, as when a man says that he has squared the circle, or that you do not care wholeheartedly for the result, or that you doubt either your power or your premises. But when men have realized that time has upset many fighting faiths, they may come to believe even more firmly than they believe the very foundations of their own conduct that the ultimate good desired is better reached by free trade in ideas—that the best test of truth is the power of the thought to get itself accepted in the competition of the market, and that truth is the only ground upon which their wishes safely can be carried out. That, at any rate, is the theory of our Constitution. It is an experiment, as all life is an experiment.[30]

5. Liberalism, Material Development, and Industrial Growth

Before liberal theory can be applied to the world situation, two intermediate steps will be taken. First, the logical relationship between liberalism and industrial growth shall be clarified. Second, reasons why a steady state cannot be set will be elaborated. In regard to the second point, it shall be argued eventually that there is no need to institute a steady state. The application of liberal theory to the world situation will be discussed in Chapter 6.

Liberalism, Material Development, and Industrial Growth

In the last chapter, industrialization was said to be a *means* of promoting well-being or material development. Material development was identified as a *necessary means* of achieving personal development. Personal development was considered to be the *end* for which liberal political society was instituted. Now the nature of the relationship between industrialization and material development, and by implication the relationship between industrialization and liberal theory, will be clarified. In addition, the concept of material development will be analyzed. In the course of this discussion, it will be demonstrated that liberalism supports industrial growth only because industrial growth is the most effective means of achieving desirable ends. In principle, liberalism could survive the death of industrial society. In practice, it is doubtful that it can.

Industrial growth and material development are contingently related; that is, their relationship is dependent on the presence of favorable supporting conditions. Industrialization became *the* means of promoting material development by a coincidence: that the Industrial Revolution started in the nation that introduced liberalism. Since industrialization improved material standards wherever it was introduced, industrialization was deemed to be the preferred means to material development.

That the relationship between industrialization and material development is contingent has not been fully grasped because nineteenth century apologists for the then-current economic system mistook a *constant conjunction* (where liberal society existed, industrialization flourished) for a *necessary* causal connection. However, philosophers and scientists (save for the followers of David Hume) generally believe that causal connections involve more than constant conjunctions. The same assumption will be made here.

The claim that industrialization and material development, and industrialization and liberalism, are only contingently related is strengthened by the fact that liberal theory was introduced one hundred years before the pace of the Industrial Revolution began to accelerate.[1] In fact, liberalism was introduced by the spokesmen—lawyers, politicians, and philosophers—of large landowners. These landowners were the leaders of feudal society. For them, the means to material well-being could be obtained through the cultivation of land. As indicated in the last chapter, changing conditions led to the connection that is currently made between industrialization and liberal theory.

Material development from the inception of the Industrial Revolution until the present has been identified with the pursuit of wealth. It has been defined as the acquisition of goods (property, jewelry, automobiles, clothing, and so on) and money or money substitutes (gold, bank notes, government bonds). The acquisition of goods and money is identified as the pursuit of wealth because goods and money are sought in abundance; that is, they satisfy psychological needs, not physical needs. Wealth is a psychological need because it would not be desired unless a pro-attitude toward it were fostered by society. In contrast, the need for food is physical because it is biologically determined. Human beings cannot exist without it. A passionate desire for *haute cuisine* is psychological because one can survive without eating elegantly prepared food. Wealth satisfies people both physically and psychologically but is a psychological need because it is sought for socially determined reasons rather than biological ones. Goods and money in amounts necessary to survive also satisfy people psychologically and physically. They constitute a physical need because they satisfy biological requirements that exist regardless of the structure of society.

It has been maintained that wealth gratifies psychological needs in order to point out that it is a contingent need. Any contingent thing that is designated as a need can be said to be a *genuine* need, only if those conditions labeled as contingencies are as they are described. For example, a baseball team's need for a second baseman who can execute a double play is contingent on factors such as the team is functioning and the absence of a second baseman who can execute the double play. If one of these conditions or a host of other unnamed conditions is realized, then the need does not exist.

The notion of material development as the accumulation of goods and money for their psychological value rather than for their physical value is contingent upon the existence of an industrial environment that is capable of supplying wealth without producing undesired consequences, such as the probable consequences of no-growth policies. For example, there must be sufficient resources to fuel continuing industrial growth, the technology to produce goods must be developed, and industrial pollution must be controllable. Furthermore, given the liberal goal of providing for material development, social and political systems must create the opportunity for minimal material satisfaction for all people.

To summarize the argument thus far, material development is a necessary means of achieving personal development, and personal development is a necessary end of liberal political society. Consequently, material development must be possible in a liberal society. However, since material development is contingent on environmental and social conditions, and since it changes as these conditions change, the kind of material development that is desirable varies. The upshot of the argument is that another conception of material development may replace the one that has been used in industrial society for the past two hundred years.

Even though material development is a variable concept, there is a minimal condition of it that is not changeable. It is important for liberals to establish such a minimal condition to demonstrate the historical consistency of liberal theory and to provide falsifying conditions of liberalism. In regard to this latter point, an opponent of liberalism could argue that evolving conditions render liberalism obsolete because minimal material development is no longer possible.

The minimal condition of material development is that bodily needs can be satisfied. This implies that food, shelter, clothing, and tools can be supplied to people in sufficient amounts so that they have time to develop themselves as they see fit. In other words, people should be free from a total absorption in the process of acquiring those things without which they cannot live: sufficient food to satisfy hunger, shelter that provides warmth in winter and coolness in summer, enough clothing for protection against severe weather conditions, and medicine to protect health. If this condition is not met, then people's lives become mired in drudgery. There is no time for intellectual and emotional development.[2] People spend their lives merely trying to survive. If this condition is met—even if only minimally—then there is an opportunity for emotional and intellectual development. Under such circumstances, liberty has value.

In conclusion, liberal theory requires material development so that minimal material needs can be satisfied,[3] but the capacity of material development to satisfy more than minimal needs is contingent upon the confluence of favorable environmental and social factors. These factors have existed in the past; no-growth futurists deny that they continue to exist.

Why a Steady-State Society Cannot be Established

A steady-state society is one in which industrial growth is severely curtailed. (There are other characteristics of a steady-state society that need not be discussed in this chapter.) For a steady-state society to be morally justified, the wealth of society has to be redistributed equitably. Reasons for believing that wealth is unfairly distributed have been given earlier.

In a steady-state society, industrial growth would be so severely curtailed that redistributing wealth would require the institution of socialistic economies in the first and third worlds. Transformation of economic structures would be necessary because privately-owned industry is too deeply committed to industrial growth to limit growth voluntarily. Private wealthholders could not be expected to share altruistically with the poor of their nations. Furthermore, human selfishness would undermine attempts to institute socialistic economies in the first and third worlds peacefully.

Human selfishness has been indicted as the main barrier to the economic transformation of established societies. Not only are people fundamentally selfish, they are irrationally selfish. The classical liberal belief, first expressed by Thomas Hobbes, that people will use intelligence in directing their interests is doubtful. The evidence for this claim is so publicly available that it is surprising that it is questioned. The news media tell us, for example, that young men desire overpowered automobiles, which annually kill and cripple at staggeringly high rates, despite the fact that educational media publicize the consequences of treating an automobile as a "masculinity tool." Young women are being seduced into smoking cigarettes by advertising which suggests that smoking is a sign of liberation and sophistication. Women are not deterred by the evidence that cigarette smoking has increased the incidence of lung cancer in women significantly.

That people are mostly selfish and irrational is hardly new information. The relevant questions that emerge from reciting what is painfully obvious are: What notice have social and political theorists taken of human irrationality when they have proposed reforms, and how does human irrational selfishness limit our options? Social reformers consistently make the mistake of thinking that people can be convinced to change their personal behavior or transform their social and political institutions because it is advantageous for them to do so. If social reformers are not led into this mistake, they are led into the error of believing that people can be forced to change by revolution. They overlook the fact that many revolutions have failed and that a failed revolution invariably leads to political and social repression. Furthermore, successful revolutions produce social anarchy and political terrorism regardless of the good intentions of the revolutionaries. The point is that unless a method is devised for altering the normal tendency of people and institutions to persevere in their behaviors, then there is no reason to believe that socialist first and third worlds can be instituted.

My argument might be countered by the claim that if socialism were successfully introduced in such nations as Russia, it can be introduced in such countries as the United States. My reply is that socialism was introduced in Russia only when established institutions were falling apart as a consequence of a disastrous war and a collapsing economy. The lesson to be learned is that socialism would not be introduced as a preventive measure, but perhaps to replace a collapsed social system.

Conclusion

The thrust of the argument in this chapter is that minimal material development can be sought by liberals. In principle, this would allow the establishment of a steady-state society if it were warranted by social and environmental conditions. However, social, economic, and political instiutions could not be transformed successfully or peacefully because of human irrationality.

6. Practical Liberal Policy

General Liberal Paths

It has been argued that industrial growth is only contingently related to liberalism, but, given the reality of the relationship, it would be impossible from the standpoint of practicality, to bring about a steady-state society. Subsequently, it will be maintained that rationally directed industrial growth is probably the best means of solving current worldwide social problems. Since this claim is based on a detailed analysis of empirical evidence, its demonstration will be postponed until Chapters 8 and 9. In this chapter, it will be assumed that industrial growth has been shown to be a viable social policy. With this assumption in place, general liberal goals can be discussed. The present purpose is to indicate the direction of the argument.

Liberal goals will be designated for the first world, the communist world, and the third world. Lastly, the problem of how these political subdivisions should interact, according to liberal ideals, will be broached.

It is freely admitted that dividing the world into three parts is somewhat arbitrary. Some nations in the first group are not liberal and others are not fully developed; the communist nations are not homogeneous economically or socially; the developing world includes political subdivisions that are barely nations, as well as strong, truly progressing nations. This three-part division is employed because the nations in each group have relatively similar social problems and/or act in concert in political and economic forums. It is recognized that communist nations interpret Marx differently. Nevertheless, they view liberal nations as enemies on ideological grounds. Therefore, placing these nations in one group is justified on polemical grounds. Another reason for employing the three-part division is that its use is customary, and by continuing the standard practice, we avoid confusion.

The First Context: The Liberal and Developed Nations

Among the first world nations, the Western democracies, especially the United States, Great Britain, and France, have highly industrialized economies, institutionalized freedom, and representative governments. In these nations, liberal political standards and advanced industrialization have coexisted for a long time. Consequently, these Western democracies are exemplars of liberal society. Among the Western democracies, the United States is generally considered to be the leading liberal nation because it was the first major nation in the world constituted in accord with liberal principles, its economy is the most highly developed, and its political power is greater than that of any other liberal nation. It would be expected that any worthwhile liberal practice would be found there, as well as any liberal shortcomings. Therefore, the United States will be used as the example of a liberal state. Whatever has been achieved in liberal society has been achieved there, although other liberal nations may have accomplished more. That which has been left undone has not been achieved elsewhere in the liberal world, even though some nations may have made greater strides in overcoming their problems.

Despite the fact that the ordinary individual in the United States has a relatively high standard of living, the distribution of wealth in the United States is unequitable. This claim has been discussed in the third chapter.[1] Moreover, as I have predicted,[2] the inequities that existed previously have worsened as the government has instituted no-growth policies. Small businesses and middle and working class people (especially members of racial minorities) have borne the burden of inflation-control policies and what are said to be dwindling energy resources.[3]

In light of this situation, liberals ought to (1) encourage industrial growth as a means of improving the economic opportunities of the poor and socially disadvantaged and of retaining the economic advantages of the middle class, and (2) work for the enactment of laws and the development of governmental policies that will rectify injustices in the distribution of wealth.

In regard to the first proposal, governmental policy is inconsistent. One act, designed to appease the opponents of industry, restricts industrial development and growth. A second act, initiated at the behest of industrial lobbies, promotes development and growth. Even though the goals of industry are often socially deleterious, industrial development and growth should be generally supported for three reasons. First, the world's resources are not running out, which will be demonstrated in Chapters 8 and 9; second, American society requires economic growth as a means of material development, as was demonstrated in the last chapter; and third, the traditional method of reviving a faltering economy, governmentally stimulated growth, is not obsolete. The third claim needs amplification.

Since the 1970s, the American government has not employed the traditional post-World War II method of reviving a troubled economy. It has occasionally and halfheartedly introduced invigorative policies to placate industry. However, the bulk of its effort, especially since 1976, has been to impede growth and development. The traditional Keynesian method has not failed to restore the American economy; it has been abandoned.

The immediate cause of the change in economic method is that growth in the Gross National Product (GNP) has been accompanied by inflation and a decline in the value of the American dollar. These conditions are believed to exist because (1) the United States has become too dependent on Persian Gulf oil, which has upset the American import-export ratio, and (2) one of the world's resources, oil, is being exhausted, leading the United States to purchase what is thought to be the last major concentration of oil. The means by which the import-export ratio is being reset in balance is a reduction in consumption. This is being effected through higher interest rates, higher prices, and higher taxes. In other words, the economy is being intentionally depressed.

It should be obvious that the two explanations given for the American economic problem are not mutually dependent. That American industry has become dependent on Persian Gulf oil does not verify the claim that the supply of energy resources, even oil resources, is running out. There may be other reasons for the development of the Middle East oil market. (These reasons will be discussed in Chapter 8.) Despite the range of possibilities that may account for the oil crisis, the American government treats the two reasons for the escalating rate of inflation and the declining dollar as *mutually dependent*. Consequently, it has embarked on a path of inhibiting industrial and economic growth. If it were recognized that general energy resources are not running out, a traditional Keynesian approach toward the American economy could be taken.

Before proceeding with specific recommendations, the status of energy resources should be sketched. Oil *may* be running out, but the evidence is inconclusive. Other fossil fuels, such as coal, will not be depleted in the near future. Coal can be turned into synthetic fuel. Other substitutes for oil—alcohol in various combinations, fuels synthesized from wastes, and so on—have been developed, although they are not yet economically competitive with oil.

The proper attitude toward oil should be that it be treated as if it may or may not run out in the foreseeable future. (This most obvious claim was made with an awareness of its obviousness. The remark was uttered because the obvious is often overlooked by experts.) Given the uncertainty of oil availability, it should be used conservatively while the search for substitutes proceeds. At the same time, control of pollution created by the use of coal should be sought. The difference between the attitude proposed here and the attitude encouraged by no-growth futurists and some environmentalists (those who despair for the well-being of the ecosphere) is that the former is optimistic and the latter pessimistic. When one recognizes dangers, he can ignore them, make sure that they are assuaged before action takes place, or act with readiness to alter policies when and if undesired consequences occur. Industrial spokesmen and conservative politicians recommend the first approach. This is foolhardy because it does not prepare for genuine possibilities. The second approach is countenanced by no-growth futurists and environmentalist fellow-travelers. This reaction is unwise because any course of action can potentially produce undesired consequences. To wait for a "fail-safe" policy is to be resigned to inaction. Inaction leads to the loss of self-direction and exposes one to the vagaries of the social and physical environments.

This second attitude is generally dominant in a people whose society is declining. Fear and uncertainty characterize personal, social, and political behavior. It is a depressed attitude and, although depressed peoples and nations sometimes survive, they are invariably overtaken by enterprising peoples and nations. As an example, compare Japan (an optimistic nation) and England (a pessimistic one).

The third attitude, which I espouse, does not overlook perceived dangers. Those who adopt it seek the formulation of policies that counteract undesired conditions once they arise. This path is recommended because (1) the *imminence* of substantial environmental deterioration and depredation has not been demonstrated, as will be argued in Chapter 11, and (2) societies advance only when their actions are positive and progressive.

In this case, governmental policy should be optimistic; that is, it should attempt to stimulate industrial growth and try to overcome possible resource shortages by encouraging technological innovation.[4] First, the government should stimulate the search for indigenous oil and seek to increase the volume of oil purchased from non-Middle East countries, such as Mexico. Second, the development of synthetic fuel alternatives should be encouraged. This move should be accompanied by the development of methods for limiting the polluting effects of coal use. Third, traditional American industries should be revitalized. For example, American automotive manufacturers should be induced to compete with their European and Japanese counterparts. As is generally known, access to foreign markets has been denied to American automobile manufacturers and foreign manufacturers have made significant inroads on the American automotive market. This situation occurred because American manufacturers have stubbornly produced "automotive yachts" despite constant exhortations to manufacture efficient automobiles. Nevertheless, the technological potential of American industry is greater than that of any other nation. This potential has not been realized in the automotive industry because of its complacency. It was successful and admired for so long that its leaders arrogantly assumed their plans were not misguided. Now that their blunder can be no longer denied, government should vigorously encourage a redirection of production policy. The industry should be led to recapture the American market and to make inroads abroad.

The automotive industry was used as an example. Other industries should be encouraged to grow as well. Industries can be revitalized through tax advantages for research and development and government-supported low interest rates for moneys invested in research and development. If industries do not voluntarily take advantage of these possibilities, government can develop its own research facilities and, when they bear fruit, can legislate the industrial use of their discoveries. However, there is little likelihood that industry would not voluntarily follow progressive, innovative paths if given powerful inducements.

It is not my purpose to propose methods of advancing the American economy that would destroy the economies of other first world nations. If this were desired, then high protective tariffs would be recommended. Liberals ought to seek to sustain the well-being of other first world nations because (1) all people are morally entitled to maximal material development as a necessary condition of self-development, (2) each nation requires that its allies have healthy economies so that there are markets for its goods, and (3) the liberal world must retain economic health if it is to compete successfully with the communist world. Respectively, these are moral, economic, and political reasons for advocating that the advantages sought by the United States be pursued by other nations. The underlying assumption is that the entire first world will benefit if each nation maximizes its own economic possibilities, while assuring the continued health of cooperating nations. If the United States produces a more competitive automobile, this could intensify automotive research in West Germany and Japan. Products from all of these nations could be improved and the entire automotive industry expanded. In this way, Smith's attitude toward competition would be verified, with the significant modification that government action would replace the "invisible hand."

To summarize the discussion thus far, economic revival should be sought through industrial and technological development across the first world. This is proposed not only to revive and sustain traditional industry, but to find new and innovative resources. Furthermore, government and industrial efforts should be made to protect the environment and clean industrial tools. In many places, government spending will increase, but inflation can be controlled if first world nations become less dependent on Middle East oil, new sources of energy are found, and economies grow. Given the chaotic condition of the world market in the early 1980s, the introduction of these methods cannot be uniform across the first world. These are the methods dictated by *rational* self-interest. Their implementation does not require transformations in human nature or massive reforms of social and political institutions.

This general approach is recommended in order to improve the living conditions of all people in society. Because of the gross maldistribution of wealth, the greatest concern is for the lower classes in each nation. To some extent, I believe that the trickledown hypothesis works. However, let it be remembered that these recommendations are made from a liberal point of view, not a conservative one. Tricklingdown works only with complementary government action on behalf of workers and the socially disadvantaged. With this in mind, let us turn to the second goal of liberals: to promote laws and government policies that will rectify injustices in the distribution of wealth. Specifically, I will try to show how this goal can be achieved in the United States. It should be kept in mind, however, that a workable method of upholding the interests of the lower classes in the United States cannot be used in other nations. Social conditions and political machinery vary too greatly for such a policy transference. What will be identified by using the United States as an example are general guidelines for promoting the interests of the poor and socially disadvantaged. The liberals of each nation should adjust methods to meet their specific needs.

One of the very distressing trends in the United States during the 1970s is the revival of a conservative attitude toward government. It became popular to oppose governmental action on social and economic matters, to criticize unions for being selfish, and to blame the governmental bureaucracy for all social and political misdeeds. The conservative remedy for big government is to cut federal spending in social service areas, to limit union activities, and to reduce taxes. In practice, most of these goals have not been achieved. However, they eventually may be achieved by President Reagan's administration.

Let us consider the likely consequences of implementing conservative policies. Among the social services that will be reduced are those that provide training in technical skills for minorities and the underprivileged, as well as educational preparedness programs designed to improve the performance of culturally deprived children in primary and secondary schools. Social security benefits will either be increased slowly, frozen, reduced, or revoked. The most business-oriented conservatives have already attacked the efficacy of the entire system in the hopes of dismantling it. It is not likely that the social security system will be destroyed, but considerable damage will be done. In other areas, small businesses and small farms will be hurt because taxing and pricing policies will favor large industries. Finally, government funds earmarked for education (especially higher education) and cultural institutions (public broadcasting, symphony orchestras, opera and ballet companies, museums, and so on) will shrivel. Industry has no interest in government subsidy in these areas, nor does the average American voter. Even though I believe that such institutions are essential to the flowering of the human personality (more prosaically, fuller, more satisfying personal development) and therefore ought to be supported by government, this issue is not relevant here.

The reason why conservative practice will be as described is that educators, artists, small businessmen, farmers, and semiskilled and unskilled workers have not developed political organizations that can compete with those representing large industries, banking institutions, large labor unions, military institutions, and upper-class stockholders.

This conservative trend will be detrimental to the nation. It will drive minorities and the socially disadvantaged deeper into the lower class. Industrialists and their cohorts will be irrationally self-interested. This means that they will not make wise choices in pursuing their goals. Were not business interests given their way throughout the 1920s? They led the United States into a crippling depression because businessmen could see no farther than the following week's tally sheet of profits and losses. German industry and business were partially responsible for Hitler's ability to retain power in Germany throughout the 1930s. Is there any reason to doubt the irrationality of cigarette manufacturers when they continue to deny the destructiveness of cigarette smoking despite the overwhelming evidence that it causes many different diseases? Industries cannot be trusted to make rational decisions about the effects of their products, nor can they be expected to use resources intelligently and in ways that will preserve the environment. In the 1970s, the American automotive industry did not anticipate that increasing purchases of oil from the Middle East would make the gas-guzzling car obsolete, despite enormous public discussion of such an eventuality. In the 1980s, oil companies do not perceive the effects of their high-price policies. Eventually, they may cripple the market and, for reasons discussed earlier (see note 4), it may not be possible to revive it quickly. High interest rates, established by banking institutions, will close other markets. When these markets will reopen, no one can predict.

Liberals should promote tax laws that discriminate between the need of industry to grow and the desire of industry to make profits that are excessive and do not benefit society. Excessive profits are called "windfall profits." The expression "benefit society" is used to emphasize the responsibility of government to assure that growth follows the path most beneficial to all people. Government must assume responsibility for directing growth because industrial managers will pursue growth for its own sake.

When an adequate distinction is made between rational growth and harmful growth, legislative acts should be passed to encourage the former and discourage the latter. In this regard, President Carter's proposed windfall profits tax, which was to be levied against oil companies, ought to be commended. Its intended effect was to ensure that extraordinary profits obtained from higher prices would be used to search for new sources of petroleum. Money that would be merely accumulated or spent elsewhere was to be discouraged.

Tax laws can also be used to attack the relentless accumulation of private wealth. Private wealth refers to money and holdings of individuals or families. The goal is not to do away with private fortunes. Rather, tax laws ought to attack private wealth on grounds of fairness and in order to promote the social good. Current tax laws discriminate in favor of the wealthy; these special privileges should be withdrawn. Moreover, too much wealth is used for the purpose of acquiring more wealth. In this way, private fortunes will be subject to public scrutiny.

At the same time, advantages for the poor, the socially disadvantaged, farmers, and small businessmen could be legislated. One of the surprising and undesirable aspects of contemporary American liberalism is that liberals fight for the poor, but largely ignore farmers and the small businessmen. An example of a problem that contemporary liberals ignore is that of increasing numbers of small farmers living near growing cities who are forced to sell their land because they cannot afford to pay escalating real estate taxes. Taxes are increased in order to support the facilities needed in the areas being urbanized. Moreover, investors with political clout influence legislators to raise taxes; in this way, farmers are forced to sell their land so that the investors can buy and develop it. Tax laws could be written to give special deductions to those who farm the land. Such laws would benefit others because the peoples of the world need farm products.

Traditional liberal support for the unionization of workers should continue. The interests of semiskilled and unskilled workers require special attention. The unions that represent these people are ineffective; in some cases, unions do not exist at all. Semiskilled and unskilled workers are easily the most abused people in contemporary society. Since most such laborers are members of racial and ethnic minorities, liberals have a special reason for supporting their interests. These are the people who are denied social opportunity by the majority of citizens and who are most unable to help themselves because of a lack of educational and social skills.

Although liberals continue to support unionization, a rift has developed between liberals and the most powerful unions in America because union members increasingly object to the liberal support for the goals of racial and ethnic minorities. In addition, liberals have become disenchanted with some labor unions because of their ties to organized crime, their use of brutal and illegal means to obtain their ends, and, finally, their disregard for the general welfare. This may be true, but it should be unsurprising to liberals who understand their own philosophy. The great unions have considerable political influence. Thus, their desires are satisfied. Members of the unions, being fundamentally selfish and irrationally so, are satisfied when the legislature or an administrative body fulfills their desires. In America, the large unions have been able to obtain lucrative contracts. One of the socially undesirable consequences of their power is that these contracts do not tie productivity to pay. Expressed another way, unions have been able to increase income while decreasing work loads to the point where potential productivity in the United States has fallen too low for American companies to compete effectively with many European and Japanese companies.

Liberals ought not to withdraw their support for unions. Industry has already mounted a massive anti-union media campaign. The hope of industrialists is to obtain legislation that will diminish the power of unions. However, a reduction in the power of unions is undesirable *unless* industrial power is comparably reduced. It would be morally intolerable to countenance a renaissance of industrial dominance. Even though unions have abused their power, ordinary citizens cannot achieve self-development without them.

Although liberals should not be deceived by anti-union propaganda or disenchanted by the narrow-mindedness of union members, they ought to try to redirect union activity so that the interests of semiskilled and unskilled workers become matters of concern and wage increases are tied to productivity.

It should be kept in mind that there is no guarantee that the liberal goals described here can be realized. My purpose has been to indicate what might be done to improve social living without transforming human nature. Even though people are by and large irrational and selfish, they can act rationally and altruistically if their consciences are raised and if their own interests are not ignored. People *are* capable of modified altruism and temporary rationality. In order for them to reach these modest heights, a persistent educational campaign and reorganized sociopolitical campaigns will have to be mounted. So far, such activities have been feeble or have been ineffective.

The great American philosopher John Dewey believed that society could be improved only through greater development of intelligence. He noted that science flourished only when superstition was replaced by a systematic use of intelligence. His desire was to expand the methods of science to social, political, economic, and the moral spheres.[5] Because others shared his vision, the scope of higher education was broadened. Unfortunately, the consequence has not been an increased use of intelligence. Rather, educational performance and standards have declined. Possibly, once higher education and the culturally-deprived student become familiar with each other, standards will be revived, but this will take time.

The important lesson to be learned from Dewey is that there are no known political, social, or religious methods that assuredly elevate the moral character of people; only intelligence applied to moral matters produces altruism and the use of rational self-interest. There are no certain means of increasing intelligence.

The Second Context: Liberal Policies Toward the Communist World

Traditionally, liberal nations have sought to induce the rest of the world to adopt their methodology. In this century, some communist nations—the Soviet Union, the Chinese People's Republic, and Cuba—have matched liberal nations in proselytizing zeal. The Soviet Union moderated its aggressive policies after Stalin's death but has recently stepped them up. China has become less aggressive since Mao Tze-tung's death. Only time will tell if such changes are permanent. There have been attempts to import Cuban-style revolutions to Latin America

(Venezuela, Peru, Colombia, Bolivia, and other countries). As a rule, most have not been successful. Since World War II, liberal nations and some communist nations have competed with each other for political influence. Despite wide ideological differences, many contemporary liberals have opposed the actions of their own government in Vietnam and elsewhere. There are two reasons for this. First, liberals recognize that the so-called liberating activities of their governments often have disguised exploitive and imperalistic aims. Consistent with their moral standards, they condemn such activity. Second, applying the sociological theory of cultural relativity and the moral theory of ethical relativity, many liberals maintain that each nation's circumstances are unique, and consequently no single political system can effectively deal with every situation. It is inferred that an attempt to convert the world to liberalism cannot be morally justified. Instead, peace and harmony are to be sought among competing nations.

Before the contemporary liberal attitude is assessed, it should be observed that liberals who use both reasons in condemning national behavior are logically inconsistent. The criticism of liberal exploitation of other nations implies a nonrelativistic moral standard. When it is said that colonialization is morally wrong, it is assumed that a moral rule—in this case, that the goal of political action is to promote maximal human self-development—is universally applicable. We have here an example of moral objectivism, that is, the view that moral standards are universally discoverable and universally applicable. (Ethical relativism is an example of moral subjectivism.[6] As discussed in Chapter 4, liberal morality is an objective theory and practical liberals often have thought and acted as if their language and actions are morally objective.) Conversely, when liberals claim that what is right in one nation may be wrong in another because morals are relative, they are adopting a subjectivist moral viewpoint. Subjectivist morality denies that moral standards are universally discoverable and universally applicable.

An example of a person who condemns liberal policy for contradictory reasons is one who claims that the United States government was morally wrong for supporting the regime of the Shah of Iran because the Shah violated the rights of his political opponents, yet defends the current revolutionary government of Iran even though it violates the rights of its opponents on the ground that nonliberal nations cannot be judged by liberal standards. The rights cited in both cases are moral rights because Iran is not, and was not, a constitutionally established liberal nation. Hence these rights cannot be legal.

Before proceeding, it should be observed that contemporary liberals are not the only group which has condemned the attempts of Western nations to undermine communist nations and convert them to liberalism. Nevertheless, contemporary liberals have popularized the aforementioned reasons for condemning Western attitudes toward the communist world. Furthermore, not all of those who condemn the policies of liberal nations are guilty of logical contradiction. Some cite the first reason for their opposition; others cite the second; still others give other reasons. (I intended to list only the most common reasons.)

Given the morally-objective position developed in Chapter 4, liberal nations cannot be condemned for the second reason. Moreover, a defense of moral objectivism and an attack on moral subjectivism are beyond the scope of this book. A third tack will be taken to develop a proper liberal attitude toward communist nations.

As has been indicated, the charge that liberal nations have used the battle with communist countries as an excuse for pursuing imperialistic aims is true. Instead of trying to spread liberalism and democracy, Western nations have tried to dominate other nations for economic and political reasons. At least, this has been the case part of the time. If the view of human nature espoused in this book is true, such action is not surprising. It is held without equivocation or exception that people, being fundamentally selfish, will abuse *unrestricted* political power. Unrestricted power is what liberal nations have sought internationally and what they have obtained occasionally. Liberals should oppose attempts by their governments to control the governments of other nations because of the corruptive effect of such attempts.

Since the same defect in human character afflicts the leaders of communist nations, these nations should be expected to behave similarly, and when they do, their actions ought to be vigorously condemned.

Let the reasoning behind the aforestated position be made clearer. The attempt to dominate and convert the communist world through liberal political action is undesirable not because morality is relative. It is not the case that one system is as good as another or that the communist system works most effectively in certain societies. Rather, conversion through government action is opposed because it almost certainly will be corrupted. I believe that the liberal system is morally superior to the communist system because the latter invites tyranny as a result of placing absolute political power in the hands of revolutionaries. Marx believed that selfishness and the tendency toward tyranny were consequences of people belonging to economic classes that thrived on social divisiveness.[7] A slave owner can thrive only if there is a slave to exploit; a feudal lord needs a serf; there is no capitalist without a laborer. Marx maintained that the proletariat would act altruistically and fairly because he tries to terminate class divisions. This is too simplistic a psychology. There are other causes of human divisiveness, as any Freudian knows.[8] As I have stated in Chapter 2, the leaders of the Soviet Union, Cuba, and Communist China battle with themselves and others for political power, just as leaders of liberal nations do.[9]

My opposition to the communist movement is based on my belief that an application of Marxian theory leads inevitably to the concentration of political power in the hands of a few people. For example, in the Soviet Union, power is concentrated in the Communist Party. The party largely controls the two other forces that might oppose it—the secret police (KBG) and the army. All of these forces are authoritarian. About the possibility of internal reform, Brian Crozier has drawn the following conclusion.

> In my view, little time need be expended in considering the alternative possibility that has occasionally been fashionable among Western liberals—that of a peaceful evolution of the Soviet system in a liberal direction; still less on the wild hope of left-wing Fundamentalists that popular revolution will sweep the bureaucratic system away, "liberating" the people from the stranglehold of the State.[10]

A similar concentration of power in the hands of a few people is found in other communist states. In my opinion, this condition exists because Marx called for a dictatorship of the proletariat. As argued in the last chapter, a concentration of political power in the hands of a few leads to tyranny.

If I correctly infer that the concentration of political power in the hands of a few leads to tyranny, then liberals are morally justified in opposing such governments. However, they ought not to seek to change them through government action. A public profession of the virtues and defects of each system is the desirable means by which opposition to communist regimes ought to be kept alive.

Given Brian Crozier's remarks about the potential for change in the Soviet Union, I would not expect an educational program to change the political structure of communist societies. The value of such a program would be to keep the virtues of free government alive to the peoples and leaders of the unaligned nations of the world. These countries carry considerable weight in the United Nations and have resources to offer the developed world. It is important that they prefer the developed world. It is also essential that the spirit of the first world be kept up.

There is no question that the United States and Great Britain identify themselves as liberal nations. Throughout the rest of the first world, confidence in liberalism is not as keenly felt. Keeping liberal values fresh in the minds of the people of these less committed allies may strengthen their allegiance.

The point is that a liberal nation can be assured of survival only if its economy and political power are sustained. The health of a nation depends on its external relationships since industry is conducted on a worldwide basis. For these reasons, a nation cannot remain liberal in isolation from the rest of the world.

Finally, liberal self-aggrandizement is desirable because it could conceivably influence the political direction of communist nations *if* the latter countries were beset by great internal strife. Vast political changes often follow social, economic, and political disaster. The communist revolution in Russia transpired after such calamities, as did the liberal revolutions of the seventeenth and eighteenth centuries. Hitler snatched political power in Germany after twenty years of military, political, and economic turmoil. The conservative revival in the United States followed the social chaos that emerged from the civil rights movement of the 1960s. While there are few signs of similar calamities besetting the communist world, they may occur and liberals should be ready to take advantage of them. The implications of labor unrest in Poland cannot be apprehended at this time.

The Third Context: Liberal Policies Toward the Third World

Third world nations are beset by innumerable problems. Despite propaganda to the contrary, most of these nations are poor in natural resources even though some strategic resources are found within their borders. Most of these nations do not have advanced technology. Tools and machinery must be imported. Skilled technicians also must be brought in from outside because native citizens are insufficiently disciplined to exploit imported technology. Population growth is much greater in these parts of the world than in any other. Death rates are unusually high because these nations do not produce enough food, medical facilities and supplies are inferior, and the lower classes live in benumbing poverty. These conditions persist largely because political power is possessed by authoritarian leaders. Wealth is horded by them and those whom they befriend. Consequently, ordinary citizens do not benefit significantly from economic growth. They are powerless to oppose those who hold political power. This is the situation in many African, Central

American, and Asian nations. It exists to a lesser extent in the Middle East.

Because of the method of voting in the United Nations, many of these nations have obtained greater political power than would be expected of economically and militarily weak nations. Other countries listen to them. Third-world nations ask for larger cuts of the economic pie in return for resources. They also desire to be given technology with which to fabricate their own resources. If these requests are granted, the wealth of the third world will increase exponentially. At the same time, third world nations seek political autonomy. In some cases, the desire for independence goes hand in hand with the need for military technology to withstand opposition internally and externally.

Liberal and communist nations often have used the needs and desires of the third world as means to advance their own ideologies and have used these lands as arenas in which to combat each other. The United States and China have used Korea and Vietnam thusly. Iran claims that it was exploited by the United States and fears that it may be victimized by Soviet Russia in the future. Afghanistan has been overrun by Soviet Russia.

In later chapters, the environmental and growth problems of third world nations will be discussed. Now, the political problems of these nations will be addressed. Initially, it should be observed that attempts to promote liberal government and democracy would be useless in many of these places because third world people are not sufficiently educated to use liberal political structures. Moreover, these people are concerned primarily with obtaining food and goods, extending their life spans, and reducing sickness and disease. Any government that promises to improve their welfare will retain political power whether or not it is liberal.

The primary goal of liberals is to require the third world nations receiving aid to institute policies that pass on the advantages of growth to all peoples. Liberal nations have not insisted on this, nor, for that matter, have communist nations. The failure of liberal and communist nations to address the internal problems of third world nations and their willingness to tolerate gross injustices have produced intense hatred among third world people. The United States has fared worse than its communist counterparts for several reasons. As the most powerful economic, military, and political force in the post-World War world (its military primacy is now being challenged), the United States has been blamed for most of that which has gone wrong. Envy of the wealth of the United States partly accounts for this attitude. The United States has advertised itself as the world liberator but has not delivered on its promises. Finally, the Soviet Union is thought to be more directly aggressive. Hence, there is a fear to attack its policies directly. Overall, the United States is irrationally hated throughout the world because it has been too successful politically and economically and because of its alleged arrogance.

Liberal nations must reverse these trends on moral grounds. They must tie economic assistance, trade agreements, and military assistance to domestic improvements in third world nations. Of course, the charge can be made that attempts to direct internal policies of third world nations is an unwarranted interference. Against this charge, it can be countered that the intention is not to determine internal policy or to determine the means of improving living conditions. Methodology will be left to political leaders.

The request of third world nations to fabricate their own goods is reasonable. It is the one method by which they can improve their economies and societies. In order to become successful producers, third world nations will have to upgrade internal social conditions so that their people can effectively use imported technology. This means that the first world should supply technology only under the proviso that third world nations improve internal conditions by improving education and health and sanitation facilities and by introducing means of controlling burgeoning populations.

In the long run, the hope of liberals is that third world nations adopt the liberal form of government. However, it makes no sense to introduce liberal governments in these nations now, because more fundamental problems have to be solved first. Education, technical skills, and health must be improved and populations reduced before sophisticated political systems can be introduced. If these goals are achieved through liberal aid, then the third world may follow a liberal course.

International Liberal Goals

As has pointed out several times, no-growth futurists approach international relations with a mixture of moral idealism and academic impracticality. They ask for the creation of a mutually cooperative political system that will meet the demands created by the evolution of "one physical world." Nationalism and war are obsolete means of interaction. The reasons why one physical world has become a reality and why international concordance must be attained have been discussed before. Reasons have also been given for doubting that one political world can be realized. Realistic alternatives that do not require a fundamental change in human nature will be offered here.

World society would surely flourish as never before if nationalism were reduced and cooperation ruled international politics. These are idealizations that might be hoped for, but, being only idealizations, they cannot be the focus of international action. Of course, if the opportunity arises to advance them, that opportunity should be seized and policies altered accordingly. Initially, more modest plans must be made.

The first reality to be faced is that nationalism will dominate international policies in the foreseeable future. Some nations have too much to lose to give up what they have. Furthermore, there is no assurance that third world nations would be satisfied with a fair redistribution of wealth. Political power is held by venal people in most nations, and they will continue to pursue their dimly perceived goals.

The next reality is that another world war would be disastrous in ways that people who possess even semblance of rationality have been aware since atomic bombs were dropped in Japan thirty-five years ago. How much of the human population would survive no one can predict. Third, the third world desperately needs help from the first world to improve its agricultural output and manufacturing potential. Fourth, population and pollution controls are necessary. The second, third, and fourth realities will be discussed in detail later.

The first goal that liberals should promote is nonlethal competition among nations. Total war, in which every weapon devised by humankind is employed without regard for internationally advised limitations, should be avoided at almost all costs. Short of certain world domination by a Hitler-style government, total war is unjustified. It should be clear that, if total war were launched, liberal nations would be risking national suicide. Their reasoning would have to be, as Sidney Hook might advise, that it would be better to die with dignity than to live as slaves. I would not recommend such a course, but I understand why some people consider it. At this point, personal decisions have to be made. Personally, I could not condemn my children and countless other innocent children to almost certain death.

To recommend that international conflicts be settled peacefully is to concede that nations will not always achieve their national goals. Compromise must be the rule. In this way, however selfish nations are, the world will inch its way toward the single political reality anticipated by no-growth futurists.

To a great extent, this goal is being pursued. It accounts for the reaction of the Soviet Union in Cuba during President Kennedy's administration and it accounts for the modest reaction of the United States to the Russian invasion of Afghanistan recently. In all wars since 1945, the combatants have used less than their military potential.

A second liberal goal is that the economic and technological interests of the third world should be promoted. Benefits to these nations should be tied to internal policies which reduce population and distribute wealth more equitably.

A third liberal goal is to pursue détente with communist nations. This requires that trade be continued and accelerated, arms-reduction agreements reached, and political disputes settled peacefully. These are general goals for reducing military tension and furthering mutual dependence. They do not, for example, prohibit the United States from reducing communication with the Soviet Union when it sends troops to Afghanistan.

If the three goals that have been indicated are pursued by most governments of the world, more unity and cooperation will be attained. As indicated in relation to the third goal, world policies are heading in this direction. For these policies to be continued and accelerated, heads of state have only to exhibit minimal rationality. That is, they must be able to perceive a genuine threat to the well-being of their nations and they must be able to plan for a short-range future, at least.

I am fully aware that nothing that I have proposed regarding the international situation is new or innovative. In many respects, I have simply endorsed policies that have governed international affairs since World War II. The justification for this tack is that I see no room for a fundamental shift in international goals.

7. The Promise of Social Science Forecasting

In the preceding chapters, I have criticized no-growth futurism because the implementation of its political recommendations would be morally devastating. In Part II, the empirical claims made by no-growth futurists will be disputed. As an interim measure, the methodology of futurism will be challenged. Specifically, model forecasting—the method employed by no-growth futurists—will be found wanting. Generally, caution will be expressed about social science forecasting.

Model Forecasting

A model is an abstract reconstruction of social processes that is designed to recreate the key dynamic properties of social processes. The Meadows' work is a system dynamic example of econometric modeling. Relationships among the variables are selected mathematically and put through computer runs.[1] The use of computers and the formality of mathematics supposedly assure that the technique is scientific.

The structure of the Meadows' model, which was derived from the work of Jay Forrester,[2] has been criticized extensively. Even those who engage in econometric modeling have doubts about the Forrester-Meadows method. Mesarovich and Pestel, who draw as depressing a picture of the future as do the Meadows, maintain that the Meadows' model is too highly aggregative. Because of this characteristic, it is said that a variation in the performance of a subsystem would be disastrous for the model as a whole.

In order to rectify this alleged fault, Mesarovich and Pestel disaggregate the world into ten distinct regions. This division is supposedly justified because the individuals in a region share similar needs, produce the same resources, or are causally linked in some way. These regions are arranged hierarchically into five types of processes: the individual, the group, demographic-economic modes, technology, and the environment. Each process is treated differently as the problem being studied varies. For example, there would be one operation for population growth and another for resource depletion.[3]

The Mesarovich-Pestel model fared little better in the hands of critics of model forecasting. There is no need to describe in detail the specific flaws of each model because modeling itself has general faults that raise significant questions about the utility of any model forecast.[4]

The major problem that a philosopher might find with model forecasting is that there are no rational rules by which variables are chosen and interrelated in a model. Nor are there rational rules to indicate what potential variables should be left out of the model.[5] In the absence of rational rules, the tendency of the modeler is to set up the model intuitively. In other words, variables are selected and related according to the modeler's instincts or feelings. Once set up, the system is treated deterministically, as if its behavior were inevitable.

In order for model forecasting to fulfill its promise, the model system must be established rationally. Intuitions will not do, because they are no more than hunches even though they are based on "educated experience." An educated hunch is not a guess and is surely more reliable than an uneducated one. Conversely, an educated hunch is readily open to disconfirmation as evidence accumulates against it. Even though an educated hunch is not blind, it does not satisfy the criterion of certainty required in science. The use of mathematics and computers disguises the uncertainty of model construction.

A Problem of Social Science Forecasting

At this juncture, it might be tactically wiser to delve into the methodological faults of model forecasting and rest my case. Truthfulness leads me to make a more general charge against social science forecasting. It will be argued that the model forecasting problem is a particular example of a typical social science problem. Model forecasters may err, but they are not alone. Although I admit that many social scientists are performing the right tasks in elevating the levels of their disciplines, there is an endemic fault to social science forecasting that is often ignored.

Social science forecasting is in most cases a dubious activity because human behavior, which is the basis of social scientific study, is generally unpredictable. Human behavior is unpredictable because it is only dimly apprehended. This fact hinders most social science forecasting. None of the disciplines that make up the social sciences—psychology, sociology, economics, political science, and history—has developed a coherent theory integrating the many activities of theoreticians or applied scientists. In psychology, for example, a number of contrary basic hypotheses vie for control of the discipline. Clinicians and experimentalists ignore each other's theories even though many of their theories interpret the same phenomena. This implies that such contending hypotheses cannot all be true, although all can be false. Furthermore, one group of clinicians will place its theories in opposition to the theories of other clinicians. Too often (although not always) a theorist or applied scientist will act as though his theory and method have been confirmed by treating all phenomena as if they conform to his theory.

Many economists assume that monetary policy can control the future of society. These scientists use precise formulas to predict economic cycles and to devise means out of recession. Other economists use contrary methods and devise different solutions to the same problems. Whole movements in economics war with each other. Marxists' interpretations of social phenomena contradict the explanations of neoclassical economists. Institutionalist economists propose a third approach.

If the conflicts within a particular discipline are formidable, interdisciplinary disputes are staggering. Many sociologists assume that human behavior is determined solely by the structure of society. Just as many psychologists maintain that society is shaped by human traits developed in early childhood. This is a typical "chicken or egg" problem. We are familiar with the Marxian claim that economic relations direct the course of history. This explanation is contrary to neo-Freudian and many other psychological analyses of society. While many social scientists have adopted the Hegelian structure of history in one of its many guises (the early Engels-Marx theory, for example), some historians have retained the time-honored "great man" theory of history. These people may have been influenced by the career of Adolph Hitler, who seemed to be a person who made history. Historians who adopt a great man view are likely to think of their subject as belonging to the humanities, rather than the social sciences. In the same vein, historically-minded political scientists may consider themselves philosophers, not scientists.

In light of these well-known disputes, it can be concluded that it is a mistake to make predictions that are based on the assumption of the truth of a hypothesis in a particular social science that has not been adequately integrated with other social sciences.

The great tasks of social scientists are to develop fundamental hypotheses or theories that coherently and consistently account for the data studied and to obtain general agreement among applied scientists that fundamental hypotheses are adequate. The greater task—and one that satisfies a philosophical ideal that may never be reached—is to develop an hypothesis or theory that integrates the several social science disciplines. When the first two of these tasks are completed, then the application of theories by formal, mathematical means will be more promising. More will be said about the success or, rather, lack of success, of predictions made by social scientists later in this chapter.

Lest it be thought that these criticisms could be made only by a philosopher, I cite Kenneth E. Coulding, who had the following to say about the relationship between mathematics and what I call the intuitive side of social science. His remarks are confined to economics, but they are applicable to social science in general.

> Nevertheless, economics remains a mixture of mathematics and something that, for want of a better term, we call "non-mathematics." We know pretty well what the mathematics is; it is much harder to define and identify the essential residual element of the subject without which it would not be economics at all but simply a branch of mathematics. . . . We have still not really identified the "non-mathematics," but perhaps we must attribute this to the immense complexity of its real subject matter, which in large part still defies formal mathematization. . . . Most of all, as we have noted earlier, the economist if he is truly to be a master of his subject must be aware that economics itself abstracts out of the great mass of social life only certain elements and that those things which he does not abstract may be lying in wait down the corner to upset the nice qualitative relationships among his abstractions. By means of mathematics we purchase a great ease of manipulation at the cost of a certain loss of content.[6]

The point about abstracting is made in considerable detail earlier in Boulding's book. It is averred that economists treat human beings and social relations as fixed entities in order to be used as variables in mathematical calculations. Boulding maintains that economists often lose sight of the human and social source of their phenomena in their absorption in mechanical manipulations. I would argue that economists and other social scientists immerse themselves in mathematical computations because human behavior is so difficult to understand.

A Useful Analogy

The ideal to which social science aspires is natural science, especially physics. What is adopted from natural science is the deterministic view of the world (which has been questioned by twentieth-century developments in quantum mechanics) and a mathematical methodology.

However, in the rush to use the tools of natural science, the long, tortuous history of natural science is overlooked. The problem of natural science was to develop a basic theory or hypothesis which identified and related fundamental postulates in a logically coherent way without losing practical utility. For centuries, Aristotelian teleology dominated science. The Copernican Revolution, although freeing science from Aristotle, only began the process of developing satisfactory hypotheses. Tycho de Brahe, Galileo, Kepler, Descartes, and others contributed to this development. Many of their proposed solutions were unsound. Only with Newton were satisfactory hypotheses found. With these hypotheses, classical mechanics was developed. The Newtonian synthesis was a giant step forward because it was the first model of the physical world that ordered phenomena in such a way that theory was coherent and consistent and predictions of physical phenomena were highly accurate. Aristotelian physics provided the latter, but not the former. The Newtonian synthesis, no matter how elegant, was eventually transformed because observational eccentricities were discovered,

The history of natural science has witnessed three periods in which synthesis of fundamental theories have been achieved: the Aristotelian, the Newtonian, and the Einsteinian. The Newtonian synthesis completely overturned the Aristotelian synthesis and totally revised the way in which scientists looked at the world. Although the Einsteinian synthesis produced a different interpretation of fundamental phenomena, it continued to utilize the Newtonian hypothesis in a limited way. The virtues of these syntheses, especially the Newtonian and Einsteinian, are that they make diverse theories intelligible and provide a structure which organizes scientific theories. Given the psychological satisfaction derived from possessing coherent and consistent theories, practical applications produce empirical knowledge at a prodigious rate.

Once theoretical coherence and consistency had been established in physics, compatibility with the other natural sciences was sought and harmony eventuated. Nowhere was this more striking than in the conversion of geology and biology to the classical mechanical view of reality. The former sciences continued to uphold Aristotelian teleology through the early nineteenth century even though physics and chemistry had abandoned purposiveness for mechanical chance. Charles Lyell brought about the change in geology. He applied the theory of *uniformitarianism* to geological phenomena in order to replace *catastrophism*. According to Lyell's theory, geological change was natural and gradual, resulting from nonpurposive physical action, whereas catastrophism interpreted change to be abrupt and colossal, thereby requiring that change be purposively induced. Later, Charles Darwin's advocacy of evolutionary theory was strongly motivated by his desire to explain living phenomena naturally and mechanistically rather than supernaturally and purposively. He adopted evolution to acquire a natural explanation; he rejected Lamarckian evolution because it was consistent with Aristotelian teleology; he devised the theory of natural selection in order to support the notion that species changed through mechanical chance.

The great syntheses in natural science were achieved only after numerous false starts and after many promising theories were rejected. It is not unreasonable to assert that social science is in a period of development. A great synthesis has not been attained, although many theoretical pieces that eventually will be fitted into a conceptual whole are being discovered. However, because social science is in an embryonic stage of development, predictions are exceedingly unreliable.

There are those who claim that the uncertainty of social science predictions is inherent in, and hence a permanent defect of, this field of inquiry. It is claimed that human action, being motivated by psychological desires, is too unstructured to be charted and understood. Those who make this claim believe that social science is scientific in name only. My doubts about social science prediction spring from a different base. I maintain that a theoretical foundation has not been discovered, although it can be developed in principle. The problems confronting social scientists are very much like the problems that natural science faced during its formative stages.

Social Science Predictions

Everything that I have written would deserve to be discounted if the predictions of social scientists were highly accurate. In such a case, it might be admitted that a theoretical foundation had not been developed, but "something is being done well." Unfortunately, social science predicting is not highly accurate.

Probably no social scientist has matched the sagacity of Karl Marx in predicting the future. He correctly foresaw that industrial management would attempt to cut costs by reducing the income of workers. He predicted the rise of monopolies and multinational corporations and noted that they would be immune from government regulation. He saw that automation would be the means by which industry would survive in an intensely competitive situation. Finally, and most importantly, he predicted that economic depressions would become increasingly severe because social evolution would follow *linear* paths. This belief contradicted the view of classical economists, who, following Adam Smith, held that capitalist economic systems move in cycles. All of this having been credited to his account, it must be added that Marx was grossly wrong about the *specific, long-range* future. The communist revolution was not instituted in an advance industrial nation such as Great Britain or Germany. When the great worldwide economic depression came in 1929, the anticipated worldwide communist uprising did not occur. In fact, Germany reverted to authoritarian capitalism. Eventually, economically primitive China became part of the communist world. Finally, the USSR sought cooperation with the capitalist world.

Now, let us consider more recent social science predictions. Particularly, I would like to review economic predictions made in the last sixty years. It will be shown that predictions were completely optimistic in the growth periods of the 1920s and 1960s and completely pessimistic in the depressed period of the 1930s and the unstable period of the 1970s. Most experts did not anticipate, and indeed were bewildered by, the changes that took place.

During the 1920s, the United States experienced unique economic growth. Expressed in 1929 dollars, national income rose from $68 billion in 1922 to $93.6 billion in 1929. Industrial productivity increased 43% between 1919 and 1929.[7] It is usually stated that the causes of this boom period were dramatic improvements in industrial technology, especially in the automotive industry, and a corresponding growth in the building of private residences.[8] This was a time in which the United States consistently produced trade surpluses while becoming a great importer and exporter. Furthermore, the United States was the leading creditor in the world. Americans, experts and ordinary people alike, believed that the rich resources of the United States—fossil fuels, mineral resources, agricultural produce—made the nation totally self-reliant. Indeed, the United States was the only developed country that was self-sufficient during this period.

Predictions of enduring prosperity and economic growth were common. President Hoover came to power promising unending economic growth. As is well known, Hoover believed in capitalism and minimal government interference in business affairs. His opinion was based on a commitment to individualism, as this panegyric, written in 1922, indicates:

> That high and increasing standards of living and comfort should be the first of considerations in public mind and in government needs no apology. We have long since realized that the basis of an advancing

civilization must be a high and growing standard of living for all the people. . . . The only road to further advance in the standard of living is by greater invention, greater elimination of waste, greater production and better distribution of commodities and services, for by increasing their ratio to our numbers and dividing them justly we each will have more of them. . . . The superlative value of individualism through its impulse to production, its stimulation to invention, has, so far as I know, never been denied. . . . So long as we maintain our individualism we will have increasing quantities to share and we shall have time and leisure and taxes with which to right our proper sharing of the "surplus." . . . It is a certainty we are confronted with a population in such numbers as can only exist by production attuned to a pitch in which the slightest reduction of the impulse to produce will at once create misery and want.[9]

In less than a decade, this supreme confidence in business, the adequacy of the trickle down means of supplying material goods to ordinary workers, and the value of material goods would be lost. In the 1930s, collectivism, as found in unions, would be valued above individualism. Robert Sherwood would mourn the death of American individualism in the ironic figure of Duke Mantee in the play *The Petrified Forest*. Few Americans anticipated such developments in the 1920s. Hoover the politician merely reflected the general opinion of experts.

As seen by contemporaries, the twenties was a period not only of prosperity, but of endless prosperity. Irving Fischer (the Paul Samuelson of the economics profession at the time) proclaimed, only a few months before the Depression began, that the economy had solved the problems of the business cycle and that it was settled on a high plateau of endless prosperity.[10]

When the great crash came in 1929, shock and disbelief were generally expressed. Nevertheless, confidence in the American economy was so great that little was done to halt the economic decline. Deflationary forces were set in motion as means of stabilizing profits. In turn, this slowed investment and led to massive unemployment. The economic downturn was further complicated by deflation in the prices of farm products, which followed a large harvest in 1928. Because the farm community had increased its debt burden by 20% between 1920 and 1929, farmers were bankrupted by deflation.[11]

What should not be forgotten in assessing the American attitude during the Great Depression is that physical conditions favored continual growth through the 1930s. Natural resources, technological skill, and work power were abundant. The United States remained the greatest economic power in the world through the 1930s. The conclusion is inescapable that the potential for monumental economic growth was retained during the darkest economic period in United States history.

How did experts react to this situation? After the initial period of disbelief, predictions were overwhelmingly gloomy. The newly developed crop of social scientists tended away from the capitalist view of society, which theretofore had been overwhelmingly defended by American social scientists.

The capitalist countries of the West did not become socialistic. Political leaders found social scientists who continued to uphold Western ideals. Nevertheless, the intellectual and social attractiveness of capitalism and laissez-faire declined enormously. Encomiums to capitalism, like that of Hoover's, would not be heard again. As the depression spread through the world and resisted remedial treatment, social scientific predictions became increasingly pessimistic.

The following excerpt from a speech made at an annual conference of political scientists by a United States senator, F.C. Walcott, in 1932, catches the prevailing grim mood:

> Our state and city governments must economize rigidly. We must keep our Federal Treasury impregnable. The wealthy may be forced to learn many valuable lessons which are taught by privation. Our orgy of extravagance is long since over, and may be for some time. We must adjust our minds. . . . to the adoption of the simple life.[12]

This statement could be included in dozens of contemporary analyses of the future of American society. An interesting sidelight to the general feeling of hopelessness concerns the emergence of the Kennedy clan into politics. Joseph Kennedy, the father of John, Robert, and Edward, was interested primarily in business investment in the 1920s. He amassed a considerable fortune and managed to retain most of it during the early years of the depression. However, Kennedy was so deeply convinced that a communist revolution would destroy the American economic and political structure that he became an active supporter of Franklin Delano Roosevelt, the only individual whom he believed could save the American economy and political way of life.

World War II brought an end to the depression. Many social scientists contend that recovery would have eventuated without a war, but others argue that economic optimism was unjustified. The question is moot. It may be that the world needed a jolt to spur industrial and economic growth once again, and war supplied this. Certainly, Germany was the only European power whose economy revived during the 1930s and its recovery was based on accelerated military growth.[13] Whatever the truth, the important point is that recovery survived the end of the war. This demonstrated that a society that utilized a market economy was able to prosper after the Great Depression. This contravened the opinion of innumerable social scientists.

The post-World War II years witnessed a period of considerable growth in the developed West. The United States was the first nation to improve its position. Eventually, most of Western Europe followed. The economy of most of these nations continued to be ruled by the market. Of course, there were considerable differences in capitalism after the war. Laissez-faire declined, government acted on behalf of workers and the poor, and government instituted controls on lending, borrowing, wages, and prices. Safeguards against adventurism in investing led many experts to contend that a market collapse similar to that experienced in 1929 was impossible. The pessimism of the 1930s was gone, and the optimism of the 1920s had returned. In most areas of the Western world, another devastating depression was considered impossible. Government controls and international cooperation in fiscal and monetary matters were cited as reasons for this optimism. Technological innovation and agricultural development were thought to be panaceas.

Let J. M. Keynes speak the words that express the dominant attitude of the period.

> I draw the conclusion that, assuming no important wars and no important increase in population, the *economic* problem may be solved, or be at least within sight of solution, within a hundred years. This means the economic problem is not—if we look into the future—*the permanent problem of the human race.*[14]

It is not surprising that Keynes, one of the key economic theorists of the century, would express this sentiment. He was not alone. The following assertion by D. W. Fryer, made in 1965, expresses compatible sentiments.

> It appears possible that a world population of 7 billion could be supported at an approximately high energy consumption for a very long period of time, even in the absence of fossil fuels. . . . It cannot

seriously be contended that the world's resources are inadequate to support the simultaneous takeoff of the present underdeveloped countries, whatever political and economic systems they may adopt.[15]

It is interesting that Fryer was fully aware of some of the considerations that would produce gloom seven or eight years later. He recognized that fossil fuels might run out but was confident that technology could provide substitute sources of energy. The population problem, which prostrates the no-growth futurist, was handled as confidently as Herman Kahn deals with it today. (Incidentally, Kahn, for making assertions that were commonplace in the 1960s, was excoriated in the middle of the 1970s.) Finally, Fryer recognized that the gap between the developed and underdeveloped nations was growing. Given the mood of optimism in which he wrote, he was concerned with closing the gap; he did not despair over it.

One of the most interesting documents published during the growth period was produced in May 1970 by the Organization for Economic Cooperation and Development. This report predicted what could be expected in the following decade based on conditions that had developed in the preceding decade. The report confidently predicted that economic growth would continue if the right policy decisions were made.

As the projections for the 1970s show, if the general conditions necessary to sustain the growth of demand, output and investment are realized, the potential for continuing economic growth is strong. Moreover, looking beyond the perspective of the next decade, there is nothing to suggest that the forces making for technical progress and rising productivity are likely to weaken. On the contrary, the industrial and commercial application of scientific and technological knowledge, and the resources available for capital accumulation, mean that the more advance countries of the world can now look forward to a situation in which, within a generation, man will be able, at least technologically and economically, to control his environment to an extent which a generation ago was inconceivable. Governments will, therefore, need to frame their policies on the assumption that the forces making for rapid economic growth are likely to continue.[16]

What happened in the 1970s that produced such a profound change in expectations and led to monumentally contradictory predictions? The population, pollution, and the third world problems were not newly discovered. The potential for depleting fossil fuels had been discussed for decades. Nevertheless, confidence in growth was expected and predicted. The changes that occurred in the 1970s were attitudinal, and they were brought about by social unrest and political upheaval. OPEC became a political and economic power and controlled the supply of oil to the advantage of the producing countries. The United States experienced internal disorders in the 1960s that turned the intelligentsia away from material development. Eventually, American voters rejected liberal politicians because liberals were sympathetic to racial minorities and war protesters. Political conservatives assumed increasing control of the government. These people halted growth because they have abandoned the kind of government activism in economic affairs that produced the growth of the 1960s and that promised continual growth for the rest of this century.

Just as economic forces that erupted in the United States in the late 1920s and early 1930s influenced the economic history of Europe during the fourth decade of this century, so the economic instability that characterized the American economy in the 1970s has infected the economic conditions of Western Europe and Japan. Although growth continued throughout much of the last decade, the economies of the West were highly sensitive to change. Consequently, experts now are entombing the West, predicting that the future belongs to the communist and/or the third world.

The Role of Social Science Forecasters

As indicated earlier in this chapter, the greatest task of social scientists is to devise fundamental hypotheses that synthesize subject matter coherently and consistently. This is the work of theorists, not the applied scientists. Even though cohering theories have not been constructed, distinct and important services can be performed by applied social scientists. Their job is to uncover and describe the processes that are taking place in the social world. They are to indicate possible social trends and their consequences, and to suggest means to avert disaster or to continue favorable trends. This is to be done generally and cautiously out of respect for the uncertainties that abound in social phenomena. They may predict what *might* occur but not what *will* occur. For example, it was perfectly reasonable for nineteenth-century social scientists to claim that competition *might* force management to centralize and that, as monopolization evolved, industrial organizations might acquire undue influence over the legislative process. Shrewd social scientists could suspect that it would be difficult to maintain a "free" market under such circumstances and that Smith's "invisible hand," which would supposedly assure social well-being, would be amputated. Marx's first mistake was to predict that these events would transpire. His second mistake was to indicate the *precise* way in which they would take place.

In the present context, if the empirical evidence were as the no-growth futurists claim, it would be proper for them to warn that natural resources are being depleted, that the population is growing at a danger-ous rate, that population is a possible threat to the viability of the eco-sphere and to human health, and that economic trends point in the direction of growing gaps between rich and poor nations. If no-growth futurists adopted this modest, albeit nonshocking approach, then re-search would be stimulated to find workable methods to reform the international economic system, to discover the real consequences of pollution, to introduce population controls, to find sociopolitical con-trols, to find sociopolitical means to accommodate growing populations, to stimulate agricultural production, to discover alternative sources of energy and raw materials, and to monitor the industrial system so that it can be sustained in the future.

However, as shall be demonstrated later, there is little empirical evidence to support no-growth contentions. What we find in their work are extrapolations from the uncertain present. Just as the optimists of the 1920s and 1960s and the pessimists of the 1930s could not imagine changes either in attitude or in conditions, no-growth futurists cannot imagine alterations that would falsify their predictions.

In expressing doubts about no-growth predictions concerning popula-tion patterns of the future, Frank Notestein, the well-known demog-rapher, asserted that the 50% reduction in birth rate achieved by the Taiwan Chinese confounded the experts. He said that a demographer would have been scorned if he had made such a prediction twenty-five years ago.[17]

In responding to no-growth futurist predictions, Paul Samuelson made the following observation.

When resources begin to be short and the bottlenecks of supply begin to slow down the rates of growth, as in the Forrester simulation runs, then in the actual real world their specific prices will rise. Men in England used to be able to burn timber in order to melt iron. The forests of England as they became decimated would not permanently permit that. And so there was a substitution from timber to coal. This is where T. Robert Malthus made his great mistake in his 1798 prophecy of population disaster ahead. Malthus did not foresee the wonders of industrial revolution. And these wonders of industrial revolution are not over.[18]

To close the chapter, I would like to quote a few recent predictions made by economists and social scientists about the future of Persian Gulf oil. S. Fred Singer made the following observations about the price of oil in 1978.

> The price jump during the winter of 1973-1974 was the inevitable result of a one-time transition from a reasonably competitive world market to a cartel that is extracting monopoly profits. . . . But once such a transition has taken place, it cannot be repeated. Nor may we expect ever again to see price jumps of the magnitude of those in 1974. Instead, as Robert Pindyck suggests, we should expect quite gentle price rises of only a few per cent every year or two.[19]

Singer quotes Robert S. Pindyck. We might wonder what led Pindyck to believe that the price of Middle East oil would rise only slightly.

> According to recent projections by the Central Intelligence Agency, a crisis is likely to occur in the early 1980s as world energy demand exceeds supply, resulting in shortages of energy, rapidly rising prices, and economic contraction in all of the industrialized countries. . . . However, it is a highly unrealistic view, because it ignores the impact of past and future changes in energy prices on energy supply and demand. . . . OPEC's pricing behavior is surprisingly predictable, since the cartel is most likely to take only those actions that are in its best economic interests. Considerations other than economic ones may, of course, influence OPEC pricing decisions, but economic interests have dominated in the past and are likely to dominate in the future, and they provide the best basis for predicting oil prices.[20]

M. A. Adelman, another social scientist of considerable prestige and insight, guessed wrongly on the matter of oil price rises:

> But there are reasons to expect that the rise (in oil prices) will be gradual and that the market price will always lag behind the possible or attainable price.[21]

These expert social scientists predicted wrongly in the matter of oil price rises because they interpreted social phenomena from the standpoint of economic theories alone. They systematically excluded from their calculations political considerations. Fortunately, they did not presume that political actions are caused primarily by economic forces. As a matter of fact, however, the political revolution in Iran sparked the price rise. To be sure, OPEC nations used that event as an excuse to raise prices. Commentators are agreed that the OPEC nations behaved opportunistically. A second factor causing the price rise was President Carter's desire to raise prices in order to reduce oil imports. Carter's attitude, which he expressed in his public addresses, was based on the belief that oil resources are being depleted (the no-growth claim), not only in the hope of improving the economic position of the United States.

Political revolutions and the attitudes of political leaders—President Carter and the Ayatollah Khomeini—are excluded from social science calculations because they are not reducible to mathematical equations. Nevertheless, they matter. Furthermore, no one has ever developed a formula that accurately gauges the temperature of the mass of humanity. Political scientists often assume that Machiavelli correctly characterized the ordinary citizens of a state when he called them a perfectly malleable mass. Although there may be truth to the Machiavellian viewpoint, those who have tried to manipulate the people have failed to notice that Machiavelli leaves out the formula by which the people can be led. Consequently, no one knows when the people will move, what will move them, and when they will resist.

8. The Availability of Energy Resources

The central claim of the no-growth story that I reject is that resource depletion is signaling the end of industrialism as the primary social expression. No-growth futurists blame spiraling inflation on costs precipated by the depletion of resources and the increasing cost of exploration for remote resources as accessible resources are used up. As the cost of production escalates, industrial processes will be too expensive to justify investment. Finally, resources will run out.

These claims have not been verified. In the contemporary world, two conditions persist. First, technological sophistication grows (exponentially, if you like) which, besides increasing society's dependence on technology, increases the innovative power of industry to meet resource shortages. Second, the normal process of environmental change continues. Some resources are depleted and others become available. The first condition enables society to react creatively to the second condition. As resources are used up, technology finds substitutes for them. Paul Samuelson's previously quoted remarks about the initial Malthus' report are relevant here. As timber, which served as a primary energy source, was being depleted, doomsday merchants predicted the end of economic growth. It was not anticipated that coal would send industry on a burst of growth that lasted for more than a century.

No-growth futurists underestimate the power of innovation. It is as normal for society to run out of a resource as it is for a species to become extinct. The difference between industrial evolution and biological evolution is that the former, being intellectually creative, can sustain the social system despite environmental change, whereas the latter reacts passively to the process of change.

As I have observed, the oil crisis gave superficial plausibility to no-growth claims. And, as I have also argued, the evidence indicates that the oil crisis was precipitated by OPEC nations for economic *and* political reasons.

Given the evolutionary nature of physical and social history, some natural resources will run out (possibly oil and natural gas) but substitutes can be found. If oil and natural gas supplies are depleted, coal could supply energy far into the future. Furthermore, synthetic fuels can replace depleted resources. The technology of synthetic fuels has been developed, although these energy sources are not yet economically competitive with fossil fuels. This situation can change as technology improves and as oil and natural gas costs rise as a result of their scarcity. Fuel cells and geothermal energy are innovative sources of power that can supplant fossil fuels in the future. Nuclear power, although potentially dangerous, has promise. But, the greatest sources of energy, the sun, may provide inexhaustible power by the middle of the twenty-first century. Mineral resources, that is, nonenergy resources, represent an even brighter possibility. It is their nature to be depleted, it is also their nature to be easily replaced. As Herman Kahn noted, the crust of the earth is rather thick and provides riches that have been only skimmed.

The more esoteric technologies (fuel cells, geothermal energy, nuclear power, and solar energy) are at various stages of development. None are competitive with traditional resources, although all are potentially capable of replacing traditional resources and of operating with greater efficiency and at cheaper prices. For the time being, traditional resources will continue to be used. Synthetic fuels derived from coal can replace oil and natural gas, *if* the supplies of oil and natural gas are depleted. Effort will be expended in the exploration of new supplies of these resources. The upshot is that no one can predict with assurance which energy sources will be of primary use in the twenty-first century. However, this does not mean that we are running out of resources. Our uncertainty about future supplies is a result of the fact that industry rarely seeks to ensure supplies for more than ten or twenty years. It is simply too expensive to explore beyond that period. Herman Kahn concludes that no-growth futurists wrongly interpret the uncertainty about future resource supplies as evidence of eventual depletion of natural resources, when it is only sound economic practice. (I am not sure that it is sound economic practice to ensure resource supplies for only twenty years, but it surely is perceived by industry to be sound practice. On the basis of this perception, resource availability is ascertained.)

The depletion of some resources could produce short-term financial crises and shifts in world economic power. However, technological innovation and discoveries may lead to renewed industrial vigor and economic progress. In other words, the signs that no-growth futurists read as indicators of an end of an era are, most likely, only signs of industrial, political, and economic evolution.

I will now turn to a detailed consideration of natural resource availability. The evidence indicates that some forms of energy will be available in the twenty-first century and that the sophistication of their use may actually improve the economic situation. Which nations will benefit cannot be ascertained, but the concentration of technology in the West suggests that the developed world will continue its economic leadership.

Fossil Fuels: Oil, Natural Gas, and Coal

Oil, natural gas, and coal are the main energy sources that are currently consumed. Although coal was once used extensively, there has been an escalating shift to oil and natural gas consumption. The reasons for this change are economic and ecological: oil is cheaper to extract and natural gas does less environmental damage.

Before discussing the availability of these resources, one overriding factor should be pointed out. Research methods are crude. They have not been elevated to a state of scientific precision. In fact, estimates of resource availability in the past have fallen far short of actual supplies. For example, the U.S. Geological Survey of 1927 asserted that the oil in the ground that was recoverable by then current methods amounted to no more than 7 billion barrels. It claimed that the range of possible error could not exceed 50%. On the basis of these data, the survey concluded that oil resources would be depleted in 1934. Actually, 12 billion barrels of oil had been recovered and another 12 billion barrels discovered by 1934.[1] The situation has been the same ever since. Estimates have run far short of actual supplies.[2] The implication of this inability to predict the resource future is that a negative prediction ought to lead to increased efforts to turn up the seemingly depleted resource and to seek substitutes.

In estimating fossil fuel availability, the following definitions of key terms will be employed. "Reserves" are the stocks whose locations are known and that can be extracted by current techniques and will produce an immediate profit. Because exploration and technological innovations, as well as economic changes, add to reserves, the concept "ultimately recoverable resources" will be used to refer to the part of the resource base that will be technically and economically recoverable at some future time.[3]

Regarding oil, there are basically two estimates available: an exceedingly pessimistic one by M. K. Hubbert and a more optimistic one by T. A. Hendricks.[4] Hubbert predicts that 97 billion barrels (bbls.) of oil are ultimately recoverable. At the present rate of consumption, 5.4 billion bbls. per year, resources will be exhausted in eighteen years. Hendricks indicates that 367 billion bbls. of oil are available. This supply could last sixty-eight years if current rates of consumption are stabilized.

However, if consumption of oil continues to increase at a rate of 4% annually, Hubbert predicts that supplies will be depleted in fourteen years, and Hendricks claims that oil will no longer be available in thirty-three years.

Regarding natural gas, predictions are also pessimistic. There have been three main estimates of natural gas availability: one by Hendricks, a second by Hubbert, and a third by the Potential Gas Committee (PGC).[5] Hendricks claims that 2,300 trillion cubic feet (cf) of natural gas are ultimately recoverable. Hubbert says that only 1,194 trillion cf of natural gas will be recoverable. Both estimates assume that oil and gas occur in fixed ratios. This is clearly a questionable assumption. Furthermore, Hubbert's projections are based on trends in past drilling and do not take geological data into consideration. The PGC, whose members are representatives of the natural gas industry, estimates that there are 1,861 trillion cf of ultimately recoverable gas. Because industry is usually conservative in predicting supply availability, PGC does not assume that there will be improvements in technology. On the basis of these figures, it is estimated that natural gas will continue to be available for forty-four years if demand grows at an annual rate of 3.3%.

Regarding coal, a survey of the United States coal resources made by Paul Averitt in 1969 is considered authoritative.[6] It is predicted that there are 3.2 trillion tons of coal left in the United States and that half of this is ultimately recoverable. If this prediction is accurate, then our present rate of consumption can be maintained for 3,000 years. At this time, anthracite and bituminous coal, the higher-grade coals, are primarily used. They are found mainly in the East. However, there are considerable amounts of low-grade coal in the Northern Great Plains, the West, and Alaska. Low-grade coal is not used extensively today, because it is difficult to transport to the main markets. Nevertheless, low-grade coals are suited for producing synthetic gas and liquid fuel and can be mined by stripping methods. Averitt claimed that 128 billion tons of surface coal to depths of 150 feet can be recovered in the United States. This represents 8% of total recoverable resources and could supply the current level of coal consumption for 240 years.

When data are gathered about the rest of the world, comparable statistics are found. Coal is abundant, there being more than twice as much as the next available resource. Oil shale is relatively plentiful. Many predict that oil and gas will have to be supplemented by synthetic fuels within a few decades. The USSR and China lead the world in ultimately recoverable resources, whereas the United States is third.

The implication of these remarks is that the future availability of fossil fuels is uncertain except for coal. Herman Kahn estimates that fossil fuels can serve human energy needs for over one hundred years.[7] Although some consider this estimate overly optimistic, the supply of coal does not seem to be running out. As will be seen in the next sub-section, coal can be synthesized into liquid fuel. The technology for substituting synthetic fuels for natural fuels is well beyond the pilot stage of development. As yet, synthetic fuels are not economically competitive with fossil fuels. It is often argued that efforts to make them competitive are lacking because industry is hampered by excessive governmental restrictions.[8]

A lingering doubt about the use of coal and coal derivatives is that they produce more pollution than do oil and natural gas. Strip mining, which will be used more extensively in the future, degrades the environment. Underground mining is dangerous and threatens the health of miners. Pollution problems will be discussed in Chapter 11. My conclusion is that the problems are real but can be overcome.

Before I discuss synthetic fuels, I will reiterate that oil and natural gas only *seem* to be running out. Despite the initial gloomy predictions about the availability of oil and natural gas, new data suggest that there is considerably more oil and natural gas than originally thought. In fact, Robert S. Pindyck suggested in 1980 that the United States may not be as short of oil and natural gas as once thought.

> The fact is that we simply don't know what the potential is for further oil and gas discoveries in this country (and in other areas of the world, such as Latin America), particularly in the face of rising prices. The statistical geological evidence is mixed. . . . There have been recent indications, however, that those supplies may be significant, and from sources that would not have been predicted five years ago. For example, it now appears that there are vast reservoirs of natural gas that lie around 20,000 feet below the surface of the earth, and that could be produced economically at prices of about $3.50 per 1,000 cubic feet.[9]

Synthetic Fuels

Coal Conversion

It is technically feasible to convert coal to any type of fuel. It can be transformed into (1) synthetic pipeline gas, which works like natural gas, (2) gas designed for high-efficiency power plants, (3) refined coal that can be used in liquid, chunk, or pulverized form in presently-existing power plants, and (4) synthetic petroleum distillates, including gasoline and low-sulfur fuel oil.[10]

Coal has been turned into gaseous form for a century and a half. Because of the energy crunch, interest in this process has intensified. For example, the El Paso Natural Gas Company is building a coal gasification plant in New Mexico using the Lurgi process.[11] This assures the production either of high-BTU pipeline gas or low-BTU gas. Low-BTU synthetic gas can be used to fuel electric power plants with considerably less air and thermal pollution than is generated by today's power plants. Furthermore, these new plants can be situated in new communities so that waste heat can be piped to homes for space heating and cooling. Besides the Lurgi process, improved processes of coal gasification are at the pilot stage of development.

Coal can also be refined. Potentially, this kind of energy can supply clean fuel to replace coal or high-sulfur fuel oil in existing equipment. It is especially promising for small users of fuel because it is cheaper than any form of synthetic gas. Refined coal can be used in its solid state, as a hot liquid, or, if the design is altered, as a cool liquid. Before liquid coal can be widely used, however, a method must be found by which this fuel can be burned with a lower emission of nitrogen oxide.

There is little doubt that the use of coal synthetics will rise. This will increase the rate of coal depletion. It is estimated that the extraction of coal will be sextupled if gasified and liquid coal were to replace oil and natural gas completely.[12] Of course, it is unlikely that coal and coal derivatives will be the sole sources of energy in the future. In the United States, strip mining in the West will have to be increased to satisfy this demand.

The Fuel Cell

The energy sources and technology that have been discussed this far are fairly well known. The "fuel cell" is a promising, esoteric source of electric power.[13] It is an electrochemical device consisting of two electrodes—the anode or fuel electrode and the cathode or oxygen electrode. The two electrodes are joined by an electrolyte, which conducts current between the electrodes. The anode electrode contains either hydrogen or natural gas. Synthetic fuels could be substituted for natural gas if the latter source were ever depleted. Even though each cell produces only a small amount of current, cells can be joined in parallel or series so that a great amount of power can be produced. Fuel cells lose little efficiency when joined together.

Among the advantages of fuel cells are that they can be made very thin so that they take up little space and they are potentially efficient and clean. In contrast, generating electricity by burning fuel or nuclear reaction produces excessive amounts of heat.[14] Fuel cells are also extremely versatile because they can be adjusted merely by adding or taking away units. It is thought that they will be used eventually in large-scale power production. They can be employed, as well, to power automobiles. The immediate advantage of this use is that the greatest source of urban pollution, the internal combustion engine, could be replaced. As yet, fuel cell-powered automobiles cannot perform up to the standards set by currently-produced automobiles, but future development may change this. Even if the internal combustion engine can be cleaned sufficiently so that a changeover to fuel cell power did not occur, fuel cells can be used economically in small, specialized vehicles, such as delivery trucks or taxicabs.

The major disadvantage of fuel cells is that they are quite expensive to use, but, as fuel cell technology is refined, the situation probably will change.

Solid Wastes

Other sources of energy that can supply significant, although not primary, amounts of energy are solid wastes, derived from refuse, and animal and agricultural wastes.[15] Solid wastes are generated by the incomplete consumption of natural resources, and consequently their use lessens drain on resource supplies and increases the efficiency of energy resources. The use of solid wastes has become feasible as populations concentrate in large cities, as per capita consumption of material goods increases the per capita generation of wastes, and as solid waste heating value increases. This energy source has the additional advantage of emitting less sulfur than does oil or coal.

Solid wastes can be used directly to produce electric power. In one process, wastes are pulverized and fed to a pressurized fluidized bed combuster. Hot gases which result from this action are cleaned of particulate matter and sent through a gas turbine to generate electricity. Another technique by which solid wastes can be recycled produces liquid fuel. This form of fuel has the advantage of being easily transported and stored. One method by which liquid fuel can be produced from solid wastes is called "pyrolysis." During this process, carbonaceous material in the solid wastes is heated in an oxygen-free atmosphere. The yield is more than one barrel of fuel oil per ton of wet municipal solid waste. Another process for converting solid waste to liquid fuel is called "anaerobic digestion."[16] In this method, organic material is decomposed biologically in an oxygen-free environment. It is estimated that if all animal wastes produced in this country were processed in this way, 10^{13} cubic feet[3] of methane would be produced, which is almost half of the current consumption of methane.[17]

Although there are technical barriers to the use of waste material as an energy source, experts contend that the greatest difficulty is the lack of public and official support for their use. Nor has industry expressed much interest in developing techniques. The conclusion is inescapable that attitudes stand more in the way of the development of these processes than to technical problems.

It can also be concluded that all synthetic fuels hold enormous potential. They are already in use, technology exists to employ them even more, and continuing research will make their use more efficient and diverse. Whether synthetic fuels are the long-range way of avoiding resource depletion cannot be determined. Certainly, synthetic fuels can satisfy enormous resource demands during the intermediate period between the present in which we are relying primarily on natural energy sources, and some future time when we may rely on inexhaustible resources. As long as synthetic fuels are being used and developed, despair about the future of our resources is unjustified.

In 1979 and 1980, President Carter offered a proposal for stimulating the development of synthetic fuels in order to reduce American dependence on Persian gulf oil. His program was justifiable on two grounds. First, synthetic fuel could supply additional resources if fossil fuels are to be depleted shortly. (As I have stated earlier in this chapter, the claim that fossil fuels will run out by the end of this century has not been verified.) Second, the development of synthetic fuels would reduce the stranglehold of the Middle East on the world economy. As synthetic fuels are used, competition would most likely develop, making the world economy more stable. A more stable economic condition would emerge because a cartel (OPEC) would not have a monopoly on energy resources. It should be noted that a proposal such as Carter's could potentially benefit nations other than the United States. Prominent among such nations would be those of the third world which have been most severely damaged by the escalation of oil prices.

Against the Carter proposals, there are three possible criticisms. First, the goal of developing synthetic fuels is good, but the specific proposals of Carter are not. This sort of criticism is a purely technical one and will not be pursued here. The goal of this sub-section is to determine the potential of synthetic fuels to overcome energy resource shortages. We are not concerned with the feasibility of a particular proposal. Second, synthetic fuel development, although technologically possible, degrades the environment so that this method is undesirable. Third, the Carter proposal exemplifies the recurring evil of a political agency dictating the economic and industrial future. Supposedly, such a practice is unwise because political agencies do not understand the nature of economic reality and, hence, would use wrong tactics. (This kind of argument was introduced by Edmund Burke in giving reasons for opposing the French Revolution.) Furthermore, the political agency would subvert its goals because members would be trapped by their desire to sustain their power. (This is the classical liberal argument against the concentration of power.) Finally, the operation of a free market would determine most effectively the wisest path to energy security. (This is the argument of classical liberalism that was adopted by conservatives.) In opposing synthetic fuel development through government action, Robert S. Pindyck and Paul L. Joskow have raised this objection.[18]

I reject the contention that synthetic fuels ought not to be developed or used extensively because of the debilitating effect of pollution. Although certain synthetic fuel processes do harm the environment, most of the damage can be overcome through innovative techniques which have been, and can be, developed. Furthermore, none of the doomsday claims of extensive worldwide environment damage has been verified. There is evidence only of local, short-term damage. Finally, even if some damage is unavoidable, one must use processes that elevate the standard of living of millions of people. These counterclaims will be amplified and justified in Chapter 11, in which the problem of pollution will be addressed.

The third criticism of the Carter proposals is based on the classical economic thesis that an economic system ought not to be managed but should be allowed to float freely so that its hidden laws will determine the path of the future. It should be realized that people who believe this claim are adopting a mystical view of economic reality. We might as well believe that a ship moving freely down the river, without direction by a captain and crew will avoid all barriers and arrive safely in port. Not only is the classical economic view conceptually unfounded (it being supported only by intuition); it is contradicted by the experience of the nineteenth century, when laissez-faire was the mode of government in the Western world. Not only did laissez-faire government lead to notorious social practices; it did not produce desirable economic conditions. As was pointed out in Chapter 7, the capitalist system could not energize itself in the United States and most of Western Europe throughout the

1930s, even though ample technology and manpower were available. Furthermore, Harry Girvetz maintained that, in the first sixty years of this century, the economy of the United States operated at close to optimum efficiency only during the two world wars.[19] Since Girvetz wrote the situation has not improved.

I conclude, therefore, that proposals such as Carter's for developing synthetic fuels is technologically and politically feasible. Synthetic fuels are potentially competitive with fossil fuels. For this potential to be actualized, methods of production must be refined and made efficient. The history of technology lends credence to the belief that such a competitive situation can emerge. The greatest benefit to be derived from the development of synthetic fuels is that sources of energy will be diversified even if fossil fuels are not depleted. This can provide greater economic stability.

Synthetic fuels, then, are desirable either as a means of providing industrial and economic flexibility or as a medium-range substitute for depleted fossil fuels. As stated earlier, although the supply of oil and natural gas may run out, it is unlikely that coal will be depleted in the foreseeable future. Synthetic fuels should provide at least a century of breathing space in which esoteric technologies can be developed. This projection is a highly conservative one. In short, synthetic fuel potential provides strong support for the contention that industrial development can continue beyond the twenty-first century. This expectation is not certain: as the author of the preceding chapter, I could hardly promise a certain future. But I do conclude that synthetic fuel potential supports rational hope.

Nuclear Power

Few potential sources of energy are subject to more misunderstanding than nuclear power. It generates both unreasoned optimism and irrational fear. For some, it holds the promise of eternal energy, since it is capable of producing so much. For others, it threatens to bring civilization to an end through some control failure. Although both situations are possible, it is uncertain that either is imminent.

Nuclear power can be created through either a fission or a fusion process. Thus far, the fission process is more highly developed than the fusion process. Many experts believe that the future favors the fusion process because it offers fewer dangers of radioactive accidents and nuclear explosions. At the same time, the fusion process can be initiated more cheaply.[20]

Fission occurs when a uranium isotope, ^{235}U, is bombarded by slow neutrons.[21] This process releases approximately 100 million times the energy released in the chemical combustion of a hydrocarbon molecule of a fossil fuel. Unfortunately, the most available uranium isotope is ^{238}U, which is not directly fissionable. However, ^{238}U can be converted to a plutonium isotope, ^{239}Pu, which is fissionable. Thorium isotope, ^{232}Th, can also be converted to the fissionable isotope ^{233}U. Only 0.71% of uranium that is found in the earth's crust possesses the isotope ^{235}U. As would be anticipated, considerable effort is spent to devise means of producing plutonium and, secondarily, thorium. At present, fission processes are being developed more slowly than was expected. ^{235}U must be used to start the fission process. The current generation of reactors produce only 0.71 grams of fissionable plutonium for every gram of ^{235}U consumed. Because such reactors consume more fuel than they produce they are called burners.

At present, the United States is the leading uranium producer. But given the scarcity of ^{235}U and the inefficiency of burners in converting ^{238}U to fissionable material, it is estimated that low-cost uranium will be used up in the United States by 1995.[22] Canada and South Africa have great concentrations of uranium ore. However, foreign sources of uranium ore cannot be substituted economically for dwindling indigenous resources. Because the rest of the world pays much more for fossil fuels than the United States, it is expected that Europe and Japan will be able to fill their uranium needs before the United States.[23]

If fission is ever to fulfill its original expectations, that is, if it is to be the inexhaustible source of energy that science fiction writers dreamed about, a new generation of "breeder reactors" have to be made economically and practically feasible. The hope is that breeders will be made to produce more fissionable material than they consume. If the program of development of breeder reactors is successful, there will be enough low-grade uranium to last for centuries.[24]

As has been said earlier, the fusion process tantalizes the visionary. It promises eons of endless energy. However, practical means of producing fusion economically and safely have not yet been devised. Many problems confront the proponent of this source of energy.

Fusion involves a deuterium-tritium reaction. An ionized plasma of deuterium and tritium containing an equal total density of electrons is produced. The greatest problem in the fusion process is the difficulty of confining the plasma in order for a slow, controlled reaction to take place. The pressures needed for this confinement are greater than any known structures can withstand. A second major problem is that tritium does not occur in nature and must be regenerated by the neutrons from the fusion reaction itself. The advantages of fusion are that (1) deuterium, the basic fusion fuel, is readily available and can be extracted from water with relative ease; (2) once started, fusion releases an enormous amount of energy; and (3) fusion presents less radioactive hazard than does fission.

David J. Rose predicts that the Takamak system will succeed in overcoming the major difficulties in the next several years.[25] He expects that a pilot-model fusion center may be ready for study by the mid-1980s. This means that fusion power will be ready for use by the year 2000. At this date, it is difficult to assess whether fission or fusion will become a major new source of energy. In time, one or both of these processes might replace fossil fuels as the primary means of running large power plants.

Critics of nuclear energy give three reasons for their opposition. First, it is maintained that the evolution of nuclear technology increases the probabilities that nuclear power may be used in military actions. The use of nuclear power for military purposes is opposed because it would result in the death of many innocent people and, perhaps, the destruction of civilization.

It is believed that the development of nuclear energy would make nuclear war more probable because the stuff out of which nuclear weapons are made will be readily available. However, what is not always made clear by nuclear power opponents is that this danger would exist primarily *if* nuclear fission is the process of the future. As K. S. Shrader-Frechette, a critic of nuclear energy observed: "The history of nuclear fission technology, widely employed in medicine and in the generation of electricity, is in large part the history of the atomic bomb."[26] Of course, this objection would be rendered irrelevant if nuclear fusion, which cannot be readily used for military purposes, were the technology of the future. If fission continues to be the prevailing method of producing electricity, then the fears of critics are relevant. These fears are deepened when we consider the politician's obsession for power and his mendacity.

The second reason for opposing the development of nuclear energy is that nuclear power threatens life through low-level radiation emissions.

Low-level radiation probably affects only those who work in, or live near, nuclear plants. It seems to me that this criticism is misplaced. Danger of this magnitude exists in most technologies and ought not to be used specially to discredit nuclear power. When this criticism is properly understood, it is transformed into an attack on industrial society.

The typical defense of industrial society to this charge is that more people are benefited by industry than are harmed by it. A critic, such as Shrader-Frechette, replies that such reasoning is morally unfair to those harmed by technology.[27] This reply will not disarm defenders of industrialization because the retort will be made that one must balance the danger of pollution against the certainty of starvation and disease that surely will emanate from terminating the industrial way of life. It can be pointed out that the strongest defense of industrialization is not that it benefits the majority at the expense of a minority, but that it reduces starvation, poverty, disease, and early death.

A third reason for opposing nuclear technology is that nuclear accidents can produce ecological catastrophies. Disaster could occur through leakage of nuclear wastes into the environment during storage or a core melt caused by the failure of a power plant's cooling system. The incident at Three Mile Island raised the spector of a core melt, although experts maintain that the plant was never in this danger. It has been estimated that a major accident could kill 45,000 people immediately and seriously damage the health of 100,000 others.[28] Defenders of nuclear energy reply that an accident of such seriousness is unlikely to occur because of the sophistication of safety back-up systems. They claim that no technology employed in the history of mankind has been so closely and successfully monitored as is nuclear power.

I find the rejoinder of nuclear energy proponents unsatisfactory, even though I believe that the safety features employed in nuclear power plants are potentially adequate. I hesitate to endorse nuclear power because I would not expect industrial and political leaders to act rationally, honestly, or altruistically. I would expect political leaders to be concerned with maintaining power and industrial leaders with increasing profits. Both would be expected to pursue their interests ruthlessly to the disadvantage of the public. But the goals that would be sought will be narrowly conceived. By analogy, commercial airplanes are safer than passenger trains because safety features have been developed in airplanes to offset the greater threat to life. Nevertheless, commercial airplanes are not as safe as their technologies allow because the profit motive leads to sloppy maintenance, overworked air crews, and the covering up of technological failures. Similarly, one might expect nuclear safety features to be superior to safety features employed in any other industry, but safety features will not live up to their potential because of the venality and irrationality of industrial managers. Politicians most likely would collaborate with industry to disguise the failure of industry to comply with safety regulations.

My attitude toward nuclear technology is different from my attitude toward other forms of industrialization because the threats to life emanating from nuclear misuse are immeasurably greater. A coal mine disaster does not threaten humankind; most current forms of pollution produce only local damage; unsafe automobiles can be recalled before many people are hurt. If there were a core melt, however, 45,000 people might be killed. If safety procedures are treated lightly and nuclear use escalates, there could be numerous core melts.

Another reason for my disinclination to support nuclear energy is that other forms of energy are available to sustain industrial growth. No one knows the extent of our ultimately recoverable supplies of fossil fuels. Synthetic fuels hold great promise, as do other esoteric technologies. If nuclear power were the *only* technology available in the future, I might overcome my hesitation. I conclude, then, that nuclear technology is undesirable even though it is a potentially effective and safe source of energy.

Despite the fact that I would prefer that effort be expended in other forms of technological development, nuclear energy, I suspect, will continue to be used throughout the developed world because so many influential economic, political, and scientific forces are behind it. Just as the tobacco industry has not been dismantled, the nuclear industry, most likely, will not be abandoned. In light of this probability, one must be ready to meet the attempts by politicians and industrialists to misuse nuclear power. People who are aware of the dangers of nuclear energy must develop aggressive programs to enlighten the government, industry, and citizens. They must attempt to influence the legislature to adopt measures that would stand in the way of the ruthless pursuit of profit from nuclear use. There is no guarantee that such activities would be effective, but there are no other methods that will obviate the danger of nuclear use.

Finally, if nuclear energy is to be employed despite rational doubts about its use, then its implementation should proceed very slowly so that safety procedure development keeps pace. In other industries, it may be tolerable to "patch up" mistakes after they are made, but, given the catastrophic nature of nuclear accidents, safeguards must be assured before nuclear energy is used.

Geothermal Energy

Energy produced by heat that emanates from the center of the earth is a potential source of power that will not be depleted in the near future.

This form of energy, called "geothermal energy," can be employed to produce electrical power and to heat homes in certain areas without introducing esoteric technology. Furthermore, the environmental consequences of using geothermal energy are not a matter of great concern.[29]

The places where geothermal energy can be utilized are called geothermal zones and are classified as either dry or containing groundwater. Geothermal zones are characterized by the earth's crust having an abnormally high temperature gradient. In a few years, heat flows toward the surface of the earth at a rate that is 100 to 1,000 times higher than normal. Such places are called hyperthermal zones. Another example of a geothermal area is one in which the temperature gradient is higher than normal, but lower than the atmospheric boiling point of water. These are called low temperature geothermal zones.

Energy development has taken place primarily in hyperthermal zones. These zones are found less frequently than low temperature geothermal zones. Their current use is limited because they are widely scattered throughout the world (for example, they are found only west of the Rockies in the United States) and the electric power produced cannot be transmitted economically and efficiently over long distances.[30] In light of these facts, geothermal energy is used presently in only a few areas. However, since potential geothermal resources are great, the development of low temperature geothermal energy would be highly desirable. Low temperature geothermal zones are widely distributed throughout the earth and are found frequently.

Hyperthermal zones, as well as low temperature geothermal zones, are characterized by water being present above hot magma (molten rock). This water, called aquifer, is heated to the temperature of the magma. Geothermal energy is tapped by drilling to the aquifer zone. An ensuing reduction in pressure causes the high temperature water to flash into steam and, then, to be utilized to produce electricity. The Wairakei field in New Zealand has been utilized in this way. It has been estimated that approximately 250 megawatts of electricity can be generated by the Wairakei field.[31] It is noteworthy that there has yet to be a lowering of the resevoir's temperature. This suggests that the reservoir is quite large. Another hyperthermal field is in use in Larderello, Italy.[32] This field has been generating electricity for over sixty years.

There are no great technological or economic barriers to the production of electricity by hyperthermal energy in areas near hyperthermal zones. It is estimated that worldwide hyperthermal zones offer about 1 million megawatts of recoverable power, 100,000 megawatts of which are found in the Western United States.[33] These estimates are extremely rough, and consequently ultimately recoverable resources may be much greater than is realized.

Nevertheless, given the wide distribution of hyperthermal zones and our limited ability to transport electric power, the great hope of geothermal energy rests with low temperature geothermal zones. Thus far, this sort of energy has been used for space heating, but with more sophisticated technology, it can be used in other ways.

Geothermal energy is also found in a dry state. Little research has been done regarding it, but it holds promise. For the promise to be realized, water has to be introduced into hot rock, circulated so that its temperature is raised, and withdrawn either as hot water or steam. The problem with this process is that the thermal conductiveness of rock is very low. Therefore, a large heat-transfer surface area must be made either by detonating one or more underground nuclear explosions or by hydraulic fracturing, which produces very large crack systems in the earth's crust.[34] The former method creates environmental dangers, for example, there is the possibility of radioactive leakage above ground. In light of my doubts about nuclear energy, I oppose the development of this method.

In conclusion, there are few barriers to the use of geothermal energy in hyperthermal zones, but since these areas are widely scattered, this form of energy has limited utility. The development of low temperature geothermal energy is technologically feasible and could be made economically attractive, but not enough research has been done on it. It could be an economically sound way of producing energy since the methods of drilling are similar to the way in which oil wells are drilled. The use of dry geothermal energy has not been made technologically feasible and probably will not become practical in the foreseeable future.

Solar Energy

Solar energy excites even the hard-nosed scientist. It promises to be *the* relatively eternal source of energy. Surely, the planet will be uninhabitable for other reasons long before solar power dissipates. Furthermore, solar energy does not present serious environmental problems. But, research on it is in the early stages of development. Today, even where solar energy can be used to produce energy, the economic costs are too high for it to be competitive with conventional sources. This will probably change as fossil fuels become scarcer and as solar technology improves.

To get an idea of the enormous latent power of solar energy, let us consider a simple instance of solar potential. Using less than 10% of American deserts, solar energy converted into electrical energy with only 5% efficiency would supply all the electrical power currently consumed.[35]

There are two kinds of solar energy: physical and biological. Physical systems are divided into terrestrial, space, and marine systems. Terrestrial systems are divided into solar cell systems and solar heat systems. The technology of solar cell use is fairly well established. It received impetus from the space program. Using silicon solar cells, solar energy is directly converted to electrical power. The problem with this technology is that the cost of fabricating silicon crystals is prohibitive. Right now, a silicon cell system would cost in the neighborhood of $100,000 per kilowatt (kw) compared to $250 per kw for nuclear plants.[36] Costs could be cut by using lenses to concentrate sunlight, which would reduce the number of cells required per work task. As of now, silicon cells achieve only a 10% conversion efficiency. Since this is a factor of 2 or 3 below theoretical efficiency, improvements can be expected. Finally, research is continuing on another type of solar cell, a cadmium sulfide cell, whose fabrication costs are expected to be a 100-fold less than those of silicon cells. Given these facts and projections, it is not unreasonable to predict that solar cells will eventually become competitive with other sources of energy.

Another form of terrestrial solar power involves the absorption of solar energy as heat.[37] The heat is stored in insulated containers and released as heat or converted to electrical energy. Such systems can be used for space heating or for commercial purposes. Solar homes are already being built and will become more prevalent in the future. The difficulty here is that some areas have more sunshine than others. For example, the American Southwest receives more sunshine than the Northeast. As of now, solar homes are technologically feasible in such places as New Mexico and Arizona, but in other areas the means of heat storage will have to be improved.

It is also proposed that a space solar system be set up. This would require that a number of satellites would orbit the earth's equator in order to collect solar energy. This energy would be converted to electricity and sent back to the earth in the form of microwave beams. These would be collected by antennas and converted to direct-current electricity. As of now, this method is not economically feasible but can become so as technology improves.

There are two types of marine thermal systems: sea thermal gradients and sea solar heat plants. The sea thermal gradient system is at the engineering design and construction phase of development. It relies on differences in temperature between ocean surface waters and water at a depth of 2,000 feet. An example of this sort of energy has been proposed for use in the Gulf Stream off Florida.[38] A floating platform would be nearly submerged. The surface water would be used to boil propane at high pressure. The propane, in turn, would be used to power a turbine and generate electricity. Eventually, the deeper water (about 43°F) would cool the propane, and it would be returned to the boiler. It is estimated that plants employing sea thermal gradient systems could be constructed for less than $200 per kw (which compares favorably with the $250 per kw estimated for the construction of nuclear plants). The economic advantage of this sort of system is that it does not require the use of fossil fuels to initiate action.

A sea solar heat plant is essentially a marine version of a terrestrial solar heat plant. A large, free-floating ocean platform would be set up. On it, mirrors would concentrate solar energy on a boiler system. The electrolysis of water would produce hydrogen, which would be transported in cryogenic tankers to use centers. As of now, this system is not economically feasible, costing approximately $1,500 per kw of installed capacity.[39]

Biological systems of utilizing solar energy have been discussed in relation to solid-waste energy. Essentially, a biological system stores solar energy as chemical energy. The task is to utilize that energy. As was noted, industry and government in the United States treat waste as a disposal problem. On the other hand, urban waste incinerators have been integrated into steam plants to generate electricity in Europe. The potential use of waste is significant. Wastes can also be converted to fuel by biological processes. For example, a cow that eats 10 kilograms of hay per day excretes 400 liters of methane each day. Given the fact that there are approximately 100 million cattle in the United States, it is estimated that 500 billion cubic feet of methane are excreted by cattle each year.[40] This is almost equivalent to American imports of natural gas. Furthermore, manure is convertible to methane. Animal wastes and sewage sludge can be combined with water in large covered tanks. From the anaerobic decomposition of cellulose materials by bacteria, a gas is evolved that is about 62% methane, 31% carbon dioxide, 2% hydrogen, adn a mixture of other gases.[41]

In another process sewage is combined with algae. The algae are decomposed by anaerobic process to methane that can be used to generate electrical power. The residue from the process can serve as nutrient for more algae production.

The efficiency of biological systems is estimated to be less than 4%. This compares unfavorably with the 10% or greater efficiency of physical systems.[42] Although physical systems seem to be more eocnomically promising than biological ones, the latter systems dispose of wastes that are now considered an environmental problem.

In summary, the utilization of solar energy, whether in the form of physical systems or biological systems, is technologically feasible, but requires research and development to make it competitive with existing fossil fuel systems. There is little doubt that this research will be forthcoming since fossil fuels will become more expensive. In the long run, solar energy holds the greatest promise of supplying energy for as much of eternity as human beings will experience.

Conclusion

There is every likelihood that no-growth futurists are wrong in predicting the imminent demise of industrial society because of energy shortages. Fossil fuels will eventually run out, but, the time of this event is highly uncertain because of the crudity by which currently usable resources are measured. Technology exists to transpose the more highly available resources into clean, synthetic sources of energy. (More will be said about the pollution problem later.) As of now, the use of fossil fuels is preferred to the use of synthetic fuels because they are cheaper to produce. Technological innovation and scarcity of gas and oil will shift the advantage to the use of synthetic fuels. Nuclear power has developed at a slower rate than anticipated. It may be possible that the technology can be developed to make nuclear use fail-safe. However, the possibility of careless use or willful misuse of nuclear power also exists. In light of these dangers, I cannot recommend it as a long-range solution to the energy problem.

Solar energy, fuel cells, and geothermal energy are safer and promise relatively inexhaustible supplies of energy. These sources of power need further development, but all are theoretically feasible. Few are economically competitive with existing technology, but this situation probably will change.

Almost certainly, no one can predict what the main sources of energy will be one hundred years from now. At that time, technologies may be employed that are barely considered now or are expected to be obsolete by then. This discussion is intended to demonstrate the *flexibility of technological research,* not to predict its inevitable outcome. I hope to convince the reader that there are many positive signs for the future. I agree with the oft-made contention that estimates of current available energy sources reflect the interest of industry in production for the next few decades. As noted earlier, Herman Kahn has made this claim. To be sure, it may be unwise to ignore the decades beyond the year 2000, but the facts do not warrant the no-growth claim that we are running out of nonrenewable resources.

If new supplies of traditional forms of energy are not found or if synthetic fuels are not developed quickly, a severe, worldwide depression might be forthcoming. During the depression, there undoubtedly would be many unhappy social consequences. Eventually, of course, technology and research would be stimulated and the world would recover—possibly, for the better. I believe that such a depression should be averted through research. It is likely that energy prices will rise for some time but that they will fall when new technology is introduced or new fossil fuel sources are found. If I am right about this, the present crisis is simply a fluctuation in industrial economies.

9. The Availability of Mineral Resources

Nonfuel resources consist of metal and nonmetal minerals taken from the earth's crust. They are categorized as precious, nonferrous, iron and alloy metals, and minor metals. Gold, silver, platinum, and rhenium are precious metals. Copper, lead, zinc, tin, and aluminum fit in the second category; iron, magnesium, nickel, chromium, molybdenum, tungsten, vanadium, and cobalt in the third. Mercury, radium, and uranium are among the most important minor metals. Nonmetals include sand and gravel, limestone, nitrates, clay, and barite.

In 1973-1974, there was a general shortage of nonfuel mineral resources, which caused catastrophic rises in prices. It was widely believed that the cause of these disturbing conditions was the same as the cause of the oil crisis of 1973—that metal and nonmetal minerals were being depleted exponentially and that the finitude of the earth was being met. Contrary to these expectations, shortages and price increases were short-lived. And the tendency that has been consistent since World War II continued—costs of nonfuel raw materials declined.

No-growth futurists claim that supplies of mineral resources are declining at an exponential rate and will be depleted within the foreseeable future. Fortunately, experts reject this claim. They maintain that there are no long-range shortages of mineral resources in general, although some resources may be depleted. In fact, supplies are relatively inexhaustible. Commentators also contend that an analogy between energy supplies and other resources is invalid.

As I have said, the energy crisis was motivated by the desire of Arab nations to punish the Western world, especially the United States, for its political support of Israel and by the desire of Arab industries to make exorbitant profits. The Arab boycott was successful because the major Western nations had become highly dependent on Arab oil and had systematically substituted oil for coal. The same situation is unlikely to occur in the case of nonfuel resources because sources are more diversified, substitutes for a particular resource are easily found, and recycling can spur conservation.

Although the long-term picture of mineral resources is bright, it will be admitted that there is a problem in ensuring a steady flow of key nonfuel resources. The problem is a typical example of a political struggle in which nations compete with each other for economic power. The next generation may witness economic uncertainty because a concerted effort to shift political power away from the West is underway. For the first several decades after World War II, the United States successfully retained political and economic primacy in the West; developing nations could not challenge this supremacy because they were engrossed in fighting colonialism and establishing national identities. In the last decade or so, the situation has changed. Developing nations are increasing their political and economic power, and the Western coalition shows signs of breaking up because of the desire of Western Europe and Japan to be less dependent upon the United States. (Iran and Afghanistan in 1979 and 1980 are the new arenas in which Western Europe and Japan are seeking independence from the United States and the United States is attempting to maintain its influence. Thus far, it is reasonable to conclude that the United States continues to dominate Western politics, but the partners of the United States have considerable flexibility of action.)

Given the political and economic jockeying between the first world nations and the developing nations, economic instability may continue for a considerable time. Recessions may occur during this period of transition.

The Availability of Key Resources

The resources that we are considering in this section are located in the earth's crust. Experts agree that the amount of material extracted from the earth's crust has been minimal. Let me quote two of the most optimistic analysts. First, F. E. Banks says, "The stock of raw materials that can be found within just the upper crust of the earth is, in point of fact, tremendous."[1] And Herman Kahn supports the general tenor of these remarks:

> . . . there is an abundance of raw materials for the future genera-
> tions as well as the present one, and that the more man develops
> economically and technologically, the more there will be for all
> humanity . . . It is our view that very few important materials in the
> world—perhaps none—will become unduly scarce, although the dis-
> tribution of the prime sources of many of them is so uneven that
> unless we are careful cartels might occasionally be able to extract

higher prices than usual from consumers, thus causing local needs for conservation, substitution and redesign.[2]

To compare these highly optimistic opinions with the view of no-growth futurists, I will quote from a Meadows' study. Meadows presents the following chart indicating the time at which various resources will run out.[3]

Potential Exhaustion of Selected Materials

Resources	Average Annual Growth in Use (%)	Years Remaining Low	High
Aluminum	6.4	33	49
Chromium	2.6	115	137
Coal	4.1	118	132
Cobalt	1.5	90	132
Copper	4.6	27	46
Gold	4.1	6	17
Iron	1.8	154	n.a.
Lead	2.0	28	119
Manganese	2.9	106	123
Mercury	2.6	19	44
Molybdenum	4.5	65	92
Natural Gas	4.7	19	58
Nickel	3.4	50	75
Petroleum	3.9	23	43
Platinum	3.8	41	49
Silver	2.7	15	23
Tin	1.1	62	92
Tungsten	2.5	27	n.a.
Zinc	2.9	76	115

If we consider some of these figures, it is easy to see that Meadows' claims are misleading. For example, Meadows admits that his projection about the availability of aluminum is based on the amount of *known reserves of bauxite*. His data was obtained from the 1973 U.S. Bureau of Mines Report, *Mineral Facts and Problems, 1970*. As Herman Kahn notes, Meadows overlooks sources of aluminum other than high-grade bauxite. Furthermore, as Kahn points out, the document from which Meadows obtained his figures states that "the nation has virtually inexhaustible potential resources of aluminous materials other than bauxite." Moreover, a document released in 1973, *U.S. Mineral Resources*, more than doubles the estimate of known resources in the 1970 document.[4]

Meadows claims that iron resources will be depleted in 154 years. This figure is not cause for concern when we consider that industry rarely searches for reserves that will last for more than a twenty-year period. However, the situation is even better than this. Peter Flawn asserts that giant high-grade deposits are found in all continents with huge reserves of high-grade ore. Flawn concludes that, even though iron consumption will increase as the world industrializes and population grows, availability is assured.[5]

Meadows predicts that mercury supplies will be depleted in between nineteen and forty-four years. This does not take into account that the U.S. Geological Survey of 1973 states:

> At most mercury mines, no effort has been made to ascertain the ultimate reserve of the deposit in advance of exploitation, and at few mines is enough ore blocked out for more than one year of operation.[6]

Such practice is consistent with the industrial policy of exploration only for the near future. Kahn cites a study of the Council on International Economic Policy concerning critical imported raw materials. It compares the reserves that were known to be available in 1959 with the amount known to be available in 1970.[7]

How Known Reserves Alter

Ore	Known Reserves in 1950 (1,000 Metric Tons)	Known Reserves in 1970 (1,000 Metric Tons)	Percentage Increase
Iron	19,000,000	251,000,000	1,321
Manganese	500,000	635,000	27
Chromite	100,000	775,000	675
Tungsten	1,903	1,328	-30
Copper	100,000	279,000	179
Lead	40,000	86,000	115
Zinc	70,000	113,000	61
Tin	6,000	6,600	10
Bauxite	1,400,000	5,300,000	279
Potash	5,000,000	118,000,000	2,360
Phosphates	26,000,000	1,178,000,000	4,430
Oil	75,000,000	455,000,000	507

The exponential growth of reserves as industrial needs manifest leads commentators such as Wilfred Beckerman of the University of London to make the following sort of claim:

> At no point is it worth prospecting for enough to last to the end of eternity, or even some compromise period, such as a hundred million years, or even 1,000 years. New reserves are found, on the whole, as they are needed, and needs do not always rise exponentially at past rates. In fact, given the natural concentrations of the key metals in the earth's crust, as indicated by a large number of random samples, the total natural occurrence of most metals in the top mile of the earth's crust has been estimated to be about a million times as great as present known reserves. Since the latter amount to about 100 years' supplies this means we have enough to last about one hundred million years.[8]

As can be seen, the problem does not have to do with the amount of minerals that can be found in the ground. It has been said that known reserves may only scratch the surface of resources that are ultimately recoverable as discovery, technological advances, and changes in economic conditions turn potential resources into proved reserves.[9] Several factors should make the picture brighter.

First, substitutes for scarce resources are readily available.

> . . . aluminum, glass, paper, and plastic are substitutes for tin in cans and containers; plastics are substitutes for lead in building construction and electrical cable covering; aluminum and plastics can substitute for chromium on automobiles and nickel and zinc can substitute for chromium in plating iron and steel for corrosive-resistance purposes; aluminum can substitute for copper in some use.[10]

New substitutes can be found in the future. For example, if the physical properties of silicates, the most plentiful material in the earth's crust, were improved, they could replace a variety of metals. To hasten the process of replacement, the U.S. Bureau of Mines has undertaken a study to explore the possible extraction of aluminum from clay, alunite, anorthosite and coal mining washings.[11]

Second, recycling can be used to cut costs and conserve resources that are in short supply. It is not always recognized that industrialized nations decrease their consumption of raw materials through recycling. For example, the rate of increased consumption of metallic raw materials in the United States went from 5.3% in 1900 to 3.7% in the 1960s.[12] Recycling contributed significantly to this reduction. Furthermore, 21% of copper, 35% of lead, 22% of iron, and 18% of tin processed by U.S. mills and refineries were obtained from old scrap.[13]

Third, through technological innovation in locating, mining, and processing ores, usable supplies can be extended considerably. It is probable that low-grade deposits, which are presently uneconomical to mine, will become profitable in the future. Even now, solid-state sciences and atomic physics have been employed to devise new exploration tools that do not disturb land surfaces.[14] This process could be accelerated and broadened to improve methods of extracting, handling, concentrating, and refining low-grade ores.

Finally, the ocean is rich in minerals. Technological advances could lead to the harvest of enormous amounts of resources lying on ocean beds. Thirty minerals are known to exist in the sea. Most important for future exploration is the mining of manganese nodules, which contain large amounts of cobalt, copper, manganese, nickel, and zinc,[15] the mineral resources that may be in short supply in the future.

It may be concluded that mineral resources are not running out. The viewpoint of no-growth futurists is based on a consideration of the reserves of specific minerals, that is, raw materials that can be developed commercially at current prices with the use of known technology.[16] Reserve availability is an estimate developed primarily for use by industry, which has to be ensured of resource supplies *only* for a ten- to twenty-year period. To spend money to find out that a resource will be available beyond this time is deemed unsound industrial policy since changing tastes might lead to a shift in product design or in the type of goods produced. In order to assess the supply of world resources, it is more important to consider ultimate resources, that is, those deposits that cannot be recovered economically with current technology at existing prices. Economic changes and technological advances will probably convert marginal and uneconomic resources into reserves of the future. The following table comparing the United States' potential resources with resources recoverable with present technology demonstrates the inaccuracy of claiming that raw materials will shortly be depleted.[17]

These figures demonstrate that the world is not running out of resources. It has been estimated that even if the developing world's economies grew at a faster rate than the United States' economy ever has, the consumption of iron ore and zinc in the year 2000 would be five times greater than it presently is, copper consumption would increase six times, and aluminum seven times. Despite this growth in consumption, modest production increases would satisfy the increased demand.[18]

U.S. Reserve Potential

Mineral	(U.S. Crustal Abundance (Parts Per Million)	U.S. Reserves (1970 Million Metric Tons)	Calculated U.S. Reserve Potential (Million Metric Tons)	Ratio of Potential to Known Reserves
Aluminum	83,000	8.1	203,000	24,000
Antimony	0.45	0.1	1.1	11
Chromium	77	1.8	189	387
Cobalt	18	0.025	44	1,760
Copper	50	77.8	122	1.6
Flourine	470	4.9	1,151	235
Gold	0.0035	0.002	0.0086	4.1
Iron	48,000	1,800	118,000	65
Lead	13	31.8	31.8	1
Manganese	1,000	1	2,450	2,450
Mercury	0.08	0.013-.028	0.20	15-6.8
Nickel	61	0.18	149	830
Niobium (Columbium)	20	Unknown	49	Unknown
Platinum	0.028	0.00012	0.07	560
Selenium	0.059	0.025	0.14	6
Silver	0.065	0.05	0.16	3.2
Tantalum	23	0.0015	5.6	4,000
Tin	1.6	—	3.9	very high
Titanium	5,300	25	13,000	516
Tungsten	1.2	0.079	2.9	37
Zinc	81	31.6	198	6.3

A factor that darkens the picture is the loss of faith in technological innovation because of no-growth arguments. If the traditional practice of exploration and innovation, which has always turned resources into reserves in the past, is abandoned, then shortages of key minerals will occur. Among those that will be in short supply are lead, tungsten, copper, tin, and zinc.[19] Although such an eventuality would be economically disastrous, even this would not signal the end of industrial society. Recovery could be made by recycling, substitution, and product redesign.

The Causes of Mineral Shortages in 1973-1974

As has been observed earlier, no-growth futurists blame the escalation in mineral prices in 1973 and 1974 on a depletion of resources. Evidence does not bear out this claim. A constellation of unusual factors came together to produce that unhappy condition. The concurrent expansion of the economies of the United States, Japan, and Western Europe produced a situation in which each nation aggressively tried to outbid the other for materials that were in short supply.[20] At the same time, developing nations that supplied key resources tried to imitate the success of the Middle East oil nations in controlling prices. Acting either unilaterally or in cartels, they drove up prices by holding back supplies or increasing taxes on mining companies. Jamaica, for example, which supplies about 20% of the world's bauxite, demanded six times higher taxes on mining companies. The four major copper exporters—Chili, Peru, Zambia, and Zaire—acted in concert to raise the price of copper.[21] Although such action does not ordinarily promise long-range success, it was successful in the tense, uncertain atmosphere of 1973-1974. Other factors contributed to that atmosphere. Worldwide inflation and the unstable dollar encouraged speculation in gold and other commodities. The implementation of pollution controls in certain industrial nations of the West drove up costs and slowed down expansion of productive capacity. At the same time, industries built larger inventories to protect themselves from expected price rises and material production slowdowns.[22] Overriding these factors was the awakened sense of nationalism felt by the developing countries that supplied mineral resources. They wanted more money for their goods, as well as the opportunity to fabricate more of their raw materials. Aware that the West was reeling under the pressure applied to it by OPEC, they saw their opportunity to achieve these goals.

Conclusion

There is no significant evidence that the world is running out of mineral resources. Even though some resources may eventually be depleted, substitutes can be found. This means that the continuation of industrial society is not threatened by shortages of mineral resources. However, there are significant political and moral problems related to the distribution of mineral resources and the accumulation of wealth generated by their use. These issues are volatile and place the peace and security of world society in jeopardy. They were discussed in Chapter 6 and will be addressed again in the concluding chapter.

10. Population Problems

No-growth futurists correctly identify two conditions that can destroy or severely damage the human environment: uncontrolled population growth and continuing pollution. No-growth futurists exaggerate the dangers and offer unrealistic solutions to these problems, but their danger signals are justified.

Uncontrolled population growth will lead to shortages of food which escalate as population grows exponentially. In addition, land needed for agricultural, industrial, and commercial purposes will be used for housing. As noted before, much land that is suitable for agriculture is already in use. Finally, virgin land will be converted to urban centers. If this continues, the biosphere—which is a delicately balanced arrangement among living things—will be upset so that the continuation of life will be threatened.

Although most of these claims are true (they will be examined below), no-growth futurists wrongly assert that a steady-state population must be set almost immediately. Actually, in the 1972 *Limits of Growth*, the Meadows claimed that world population should be stabilized by 1975.[1] They realized the improbability of achieving this state of affairs so they recommended minimal population growth in this century.[2] As will be seen, the most directly threatening consequence of population growth, scarcity of food, has been alleviated by the green revolution. Other dangers have also been mitigated by technological advances. I will argue that population stabilization probably cannot take place until the middle of the twenty-first century. However, movement toward controlled population growth is essential to human well-being and should be (and is being) pursued.

The other great problem, pollution, attacks both human health and the biosphere. Intense pollution causes disease, may sterilize entire populations, and may produce genetic defects in future generations. The potential effect on the biosphere is two-fold: the atmosphere may be so altered that the planet may become inhospitable to life, or the natural environment may be so transformed that the balance among life forms will be upset.

Unfortunately, distortions of the dangers of pollution abound. There is no concrete evidence that human beings are being poisoned on a massive scale. In most cases, the threats to human health are local. For example, radiation fallout from nuclear power has produced ill health in areas where bombs were dropped or where nuclear power is being commercially developed. Warnings of a "green house" effect that will produce worldwide flooding or warnings of atmospheric transformations that will bring on another ice age are premature. Evidence indicates that world temperature has changed very little in this century, although it has changed. What the long-range consequences of escalating temperatures will be is speculative.

Let it be clear, I believe that no-growth futurists justifiably warn us about the population explosion and pollution intensification. Undesired consequences *can be demonstrated. Aggressive remedial action ought to be taken for the good of humankind.* Nevertheless, I object to overstating the dangers because misrepresentation is morally reprehensible. Furthermore, it obscures the literal truth because opponents will focus debate on the overstatements and, if the opponents are dishonest, will claim victory for their cause when they have shown the overstatements. In other words, the credibility of those who overstate will be destroyed. I seek the truth, nothing more and nothing less. This search will show that rationality requires population and pollution control but that neither condition is a cause for panic. In regard to pollution, no one can be sure how much pollution the human organism and the environment can tolerate. It is not known with anything approximating certainty what kinds of pollution are most threatening to human health and the physical environment. But, it is known with as much certainty as human beings can attain, that life and the environment have limitations that are being broached. Environmental monitoring and controlled growth of these factors are essential.

Because of the length of these topics, this chapter will be limited to a discussion of population. Chapter 11 will be concerned with the effects of pollution.

The Problem of Population

Currently, 3 billion people inhabit the earth. It is estimated that this figure will double by the turn of the century. If people were evenly distributed throughout the world, 50 people would live on every square mile of earth.[3] If this were so, then there would be 100 people per square mile by the turn of the century. Unfortunately, population distribution is uneven. Java, the most densely populated region, contains 1,140 people per square mile; Belgium has 773 people per square mile; and the Middle Atlantic states and New England had 270.[4] The Peoples Republic of China is the most populous nation. Because it is the policy of Communist China to give little information to the outside world, the exact population figure is in doubt. Nevertheless, it has been estimated that the population of China stood at 822 million in 1975.[5] This figure· was reached by using the United Nations' medium variant estimate. In 1975, there were 608 million people in India, the world's second most populous country.[6] In the same year, the population of Europe was estimated to be 718 million, with 254 million living in the USSR.[7] The population of the United States was said to be 213 million.[8]

The distribution of population is uneven for a number of reasons. The most important is that some land is more suitable for habitation than other land. Antarctica contains 5.1 million square miles of land, but is too cold to sustain large populations; the Sahara Desert, which is hot and barren, covers 3 million square miles of land.[9] Two-thirds of the world's people live on 4.2 million square miles of land. This is about 7.3% of the total land surface of the earth.[10]

Population has grown at such a staggering rate because the birth rate far exceeds the death rate. In earlier times, diseases (the plague, cholera, smallpox, and malaria) kept the world population relatively stable. Population increased in Europe in the eighteenth century when the plague ceased to ravage the continent. During the same period, agricultural production made considerable gains, and malnutrition decreased as a consequence. By the beginning of the twentieth century, life expectancy had risen dramatically in Europe. Whereas life expectancy in Europe was 40 years in the early nineteenth century, it approached 60 years at the turn of the century.[11] Now, life expectancy has risen to 72 years in Europe and North America. Contrary to popular belief, medical science did not make the main contribution to this change. Rather, it was accounted for by improved sanitation, cleaner water, better housing, and more adequate supplies of food.[12]

It can be said, then, that the growth of population is caused by dramatic increases in life expectancy and dramatic decreases in death rates. Overall, world population is growing at an annual rate of 1.8%.[13] Currently, the natural increase in population is estimated by the United Nations Department of Economic and Social Affairs to be approximately 25 per 1,000.[14] This figure is reached by subtracting the death rate (13 per 1,000) from the birth rate (38 per 1,000).

In general, the greatest population growth has taken place in the countries least capable of sustaining increased population. The following table indicates these differences.[15]

Vital Indices of Major Regions, 1965-1970
(As estimated by U.N. Population Division)
Annual Rates per 1,000 of population

	Birth	Death	Natural Increase	Gross Reproduction Rates	Expectation of Life at Birth
World Total	33.8	14.0	19.8	2.3	53
More Developed Regions	18.6	9.1	9.5	1.3	70
Less Developed Regions	40.6	16.1	24.5	2.7	50
East Asia	31.5	14.0	17.5	2.0	52
South Asia	44.3	16.8	27.5	3.0	49
Africa	46.8	21.3	25.5	3.1	43
Latin America	38.4	10.0	28.4	2.7	60

The following graph indicates the extent to which less developed nations have increased their populations relative to the developed nations of the world and what a continuation of the same birth rates would mean for the world population by the year 2020.[16]

These figures support one of the important contentions of no-growth futurists—that current population trends, if continued, will lead to an escalating widening of the gap between rich and poor nations. This follows because every industrial advance made by developing nations will be offset by the need to produce more food and goods. Escalating prices will be inevitable. The fear is that the poor will be unable to escape poverty.

Despite the gravity of the problem, there are two reasons for hope. First, the green revolution is providing increased quantities of food for developing as well as developed countries. Second, significant advances are being made in controlling population growth in most parts of the world. It is probable that the world population will reach between 6 billion and 7 billion by the turn of the century. Although a steady-state population will eventually have to be set, world society probably can adjust to the problems ahead. As W. D. Borrie asserts,

Perhaps mankind does at least stand close to the brink of that ultimate reality foreshadowed by Malthus. Yet having achieved so much by increasing food, by eliminating disease, by increasing life spans to levels never before achieved, it is hard to believe that man cannot again re-adapt to prevent his own self-destruction through both demographic and economic profligacy.[17]

One of the primary reasons for overpopulation is that human beings have extended their life span. From 1905 to 1975, death rates decreased from 30 per thousand to 12 per thousand.[18] India's life expectancy, for example, went from 30 years in the 1930s to 47 years in 1972.[19] Latin America, the Caribbean Islands, and East Asia have reduced death rates to levels that are commensurate with those of North America and Europe. Only Africa is lagging significantly behind. The death rate there remains 21 per 1,000.[20]

The extreme pessimism of no-growth futurists is revealed by their unwillingness to recognize that reducing the death rate and extending life expectancy are great achievements. However, as I have said before, in an age of pessimism, nothing is viewed as grounds for happiness by those who express the prevailing attitude. Because no-growth futurism is the doctrine of despair, it is readily accepted. The secret of success of no-growth futurists is that they find a flaw in every diamond.

WORLD POPULATION GROWTH, 1970-2020

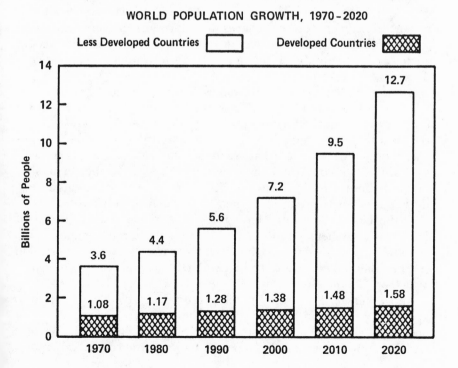

Population in the Developed World

Thus far, it has been noted that population increases have been brought about by extending life expectancy and decreasing the death rate. If these were the only factors related to population size, then the industrialized nations of the world would have the largest populations since their life expectancy is the highest in the world. In contrast, the life expectancy in Oceania is 68 years, that in the Caribbean Islands is 64, that is Latin America is 56, that in Asia is 56, that in the Near East is 54, and that in Africa is 45.[21] However, once a nation is industrialized, there is a strong tendency for the birth rate to decline. In the industrialized West, for example, the birth rate has fallen to about 2.2 to 2.7 per family. This is half of the average family size of the early 1900s.[22] After 1880, there was a consistent tendency for family size to decline as the Industrial Revolution proceeded.

There is a strong correlation between affluence (which came with the Industrial Revolution) and reproductive rates. Most likely, poor families have little to be proud of except their fecundity. Families who have acquired wealth and whose members have been educated probably value goals other than reproductive ability. The fact that more women are engaged in careers further reduces the desire for children. Because of the emerging role of women in industrial society, marriages take place at a later age, which reduces the time during which women can bear children.

Originally, the declining birth rate was most apparent in non-Roman Catholic affluent, industrial nations. The reason for the higher birth rates in Roman Catholic countries was almost certainly the policy of the religious hierarchy. Surprisingly, industrialized Roman Catholic countries now show birth rates that are among the lowest. This is especially true of Catholic countries in Southern and Eastern Europe.[23] This shift can be accounted for by the desires of the people of these nations to reap the rewards of industrialism, as their Protestant counterparts have.

In the United States, the birth rate was 15.8 in the first quarter of 1972. This rate held firm through 1975. The birth rate for these years was lower than the lowest birth rate in the worst year of the depression (18.4 in 1936). By contrast, the highest birth rate registered after World War II was 25.3 in 1957.[24]

Altogether, birth rates in the industrial world have been reduced to about 2.5 per woman. This implies a growth rate for the population of about 1%—if the population remains stable. But since many Western nations admit immigrants from poorer nations (who consistently reproduce at a higher rate), the actual birth rate will be higher. To reach "zero population growth" in the industrial world would entail reducing the number of children to about 1.5 per couple, a figure that is attainable.[25] But it is unlikely that zero population growth will be attained by the turn of the century. The United States, for example, probably will go from 213.6 million people in 1975 to 262 million people in 2000.[26]

Such growth patterns should not be upsetting. Surely, they do not reflect that our world situation is ideal. People do not do what is the best that can be done in every context. This is hardly new information. The evidence shows, however, that both conscious planning and unconscious factors operate to reduce growth rates to manageable levels. This fact is obscured by the prevailing resolute pessimism. The unconscious cause of declining growth figures is that wealth produces other interests which replace the value of childbearing. The conscious causes are the new image of women which leads them to seek fulfillment in nonparental roles, and an awareness of the growth problem, which leads educated, socially conscious people to be satisfied with smaller families. The last factor cannot be overestimated. It is striking that Western European countries and the United States showed significant birth rate declines during the 1970s, just after the problem of population growth became publicized.

Population in the Developing World

The situation in the developing world is neither as bright as it is in the industrialized world nor as dim as no-growth futurists suggest. It is estimated that the population of the developing world will double in about thirty years.[27] Since most of the people in the developing world live in areas that are not highly industrialized and that do not produce sufficient food, malnutrition is common. The pressure to find more food sources may intensify as the century moves to a close. On the other hand, the reason for the increase in population is that the death rate has declined and life expectancy has increased in developing nations. It is the case, then, that good has brought an attending evil. As shall be seen, however, the situation is not hopeless because these nations are making progress in controlling population growth. The general problem seems to be that the advances made in extending life and reducing the death rate have not been accompanied by significant advances in education, industrialization, and agriculture.

Population growth is most extreme in India, Pakistan, Bangladesh, and Indonesia. For example, the growth rate in India exceeds 2.5%.

From 1921 to 1971, the population increased from 306 million to 570 million.[28] Since that time, population growth has slowed to 2% annually.[29] The reasons for this slowdown will be examined later. In Africa, growth problems are severe because unstable governments prevent adequate planning. In Latin America, even though the population continues to grow at a high rate, there is great potential for economic development as natural resources are exploited. Furthermore, the number of people per square mile is relatively low.

The situation in the developing world is not so grim as no-growth futurists claim because the green revolution will make it possible to feed much of the population. In addition, the peoples of these nations have instituted measures to counteract population growth.

Measures Being Taken to Control Population Growth

The goals of no-growth futurists are probably unattainable. Population will double before the century is over, but this fact will be offset by economic growth and agricultural development. Zero population growth eventually must be reached, but not in the near future. On the other hand, slowing population growth is essential, and much has been done along these lines. The situation may be summed up as requiring population controls, but as agricultural and industrial growth continue the world can tolerate a larger population. In other words, one of the very processes that no-growth futurists seek to slow down, industrial development, is one of the means by which the needs of growing populations can be met.

Furthermore, approximately two-thirds of the world's nations instituted programs to control population in the 1970s. Between 1965 and 1975, the world birth rate dropped faster than the death rate. A decline in birth rate was apparent in Asia, Latin America, the Near East, and the Caribbean Islands.[30]

Specifically, the world birth rate declined from an average of 34 per 1,000 in 1965 to 30 per 1,000 in 1974. These decreases were experienced in 127 countries. The United States went from 19 per 1,000 to 15 per 1,000; Canada from 21 per 1,000 to 15 per 1,000; Europe from 18 per 1,000 to 16 per 1,000; Southeast Asia from 44 per 1,000 to 38 per 1,000; South Asia from 44 per 1,000 to 38 per 1,000; East Asia from 33 per 1,000 to 26 per 1,000; and Latin America from 39 per 1,000 to 37 per 1,000.[31]

Figures 1 and 2 tell the story of population in this century. What is interesting in Figure 1 is that the sharp decline in death rate produced a

Fig. 1. VITAL INDICES OF MAJOR REGIONS, 1965-1970
(As estimated by U.N. Population Division)

Annual rates per 1000 of population

	Birth	Death	Natural Increase	Gross Reproduction Rates	Expectation of Life at Birth
World Total	33.8	14.0	19.8	2.3	53
More Developed Regions	18.6	9.1	9.5	1.3	70
Less Developed Regions	40.6	16.1	24.5	2.7	50
East Asia	31.5	14.0	17.5	2.0	52
South Asia	44.3	16.8	27.5	3.0	49
Africa	46.8	21.3	25.5	3.1	43
Latin America	38.4	10.1	28.4	2.7	60

corresponding increase in population growth rate despite a lower birth rate. Since 1965, the birth rate began to decline quite rapidly so that the population growth rates declined for the first time since 1915.[32] Figure 2 measures the natural rate of increase for major regions of the world between 1965 and 1974. It indicates what we may expect in a future in which the world has been made aware of the growth problem.[33]

A decline in birth rate has been noted in the most populous countries. Figure 3 shows the relevant data.[34]

In considering individual nations, the case of India is especially interesting. Here, we see clear differences among the hopes of idealistic reformers, stereotypical views, and mundane reality. The idealists set

Fig. 2. Rates of Natural Increase for Major Regions and the World

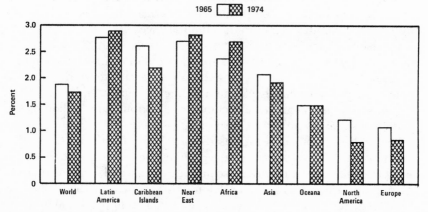

Source: Population Reference Bureau

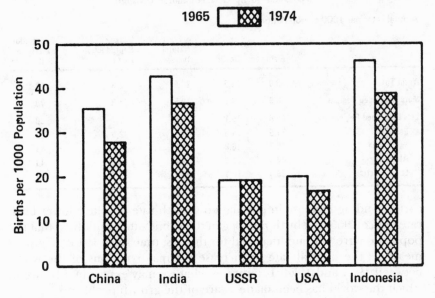

Fig. 3. Birth Rates in the Five Most Populous Countries of the World

Source: Population Reference Bureau

goals that cannot be reached because their goals run up against complicated human nature. Stereotypical views simplify reality so that people
and situations are perceived to be either better or worse than they are.
Because the idealistic and stereotypical views are dramatic and simple,
they become fodder for ideologues and popular writers. They are ready
sources for encomiums, complaints, and predictions. This is why many
predictions turn into fiction, rather than science.

According to stereotypical views, the situation in India is hopeless.
Starvation is rampant; population growth is out of control; the economy
is stagnant. The idealists have set goals to extricate India from its
dangerous position, but they cannot be met. Actually, India's situation
has improved in regard to agriculture and population, although this
country is still in a dangerous position.

The Indian population increased from 306 million in 1921 to 570
million in 1971. This produced a very high human-land ratio (400 persons per square mile). In order to counteract this trend, a national family
planning program was set in 1955 and implemented in 1963. The goal
was to reduce the birth rate from 41 per 1,000 to 25 per 1,000 by 1973.
A United Nations Technical Assistance Mission was invited to observe

the situation and recommend a means of meeting these figures. The following measures were proposed: extending male sterilization, issuing a greater number of traditional contraceptives to the people, and increasing the number of clinics and information services throughout the country to advertise the family planning program. The UN mission set targets of reducing growth rates from 2.4% in 1966 to 1.6% in 1975 to less than 1.0% by 1985. In effect, if 85 billion births were prevented by 1975, the birth rate would have been reduced to the desired 25 per 1,000 by 1975.[35] The complexity of the social structure doomed these plans to failure. The administrative system, like almost all such systems, did not work smoothly. The people, like all human beings, were not as susceptible to propaganda as officials thought.

Even though the desired goals were not reached, significant progress was made. The Indian Congress liberalized abortion laws in 1971. In some states—the Punjab, Southern Kerala, and Rajasthan—birth rates may be declining. Some projections suggest that 3 million to 4 million births may be prevented.[36] By 1974, the birth rate fell to 35 per 1,000. This figure was offset somewhat by the fact that longevity had increased to 50 years by 1974. At that time, the population was growing at a rate of 2.0%. New government policies hope to reduce the annual growth rate 1.4% by 1986. So far, sterilization has been the mainstay of the family planning program. Government officials estimate that 14% of the population of reproductive age use some form of contraception. Birth rates have declined more in cities than in rural areas. Future programs will be aimed at rural areas.[37]

During this period, India has made impressive strides agriculturally and industrially. However, Herman Kahn maintains that not enough emphasis has been placed on agricultural growth in official government policy. Instead, the government has expended its efforts in promoting capital-intensive industries such as steel, developing nuclear energy, and strengthening national defense. In 1972-1973, India's defense expenditures comprised the largest item in the national budget, amounting to one-third of the total. Agricultural expenditures, on the other hand, declined from $1.1 billion in 1971 to $850 million in 1974.[38] Fortunately, since Kahn wrote, new policies have been instituted in India. These resulted in a record grain crop in 1976.[39]

The population problem in India does not seem to be insurmountable. Although a steady-state population probably will not be achieved until 2020, the population growth rate has been slowed, and the rate of decline should increase significantly by the year 2000. Population increases can be offset by improvements in agriculture and industry. As of now, most of India's inhabitants merely subsist. The situation might improve, but it is unrealistic to expect income levels to approach those in the developed world in the foreseeable future. Malnutrition will continue as well, but the incidence of starvation should be lower than it is today.

The Politics of Population

The United Nations designated 1974 as World Population Year. In August of that year, a conference held in Bucharest, Romania was devoted to devising a world plan for solving the population problem. One hundred-and-thirty-six nations sent delegates to the conference. There was considerable debate over the causes of the problem and the methods that could best solve it. Developing nations noting that economic and industrial development produces lower birth rates, argued that the developed world ought to spend time and money in improving the economies of developing nations. Developed nations, which had already channeled a considerable amount of money into developing poorer nations, argued that development policies were ineffective when population growth proceeded unchecked. These two views were integrated in paragraph 14 of the World Population Plan of Action:

> Population and development are interrelated: population variables influence development variables and are also influenced by them; thus the formulation of a World Population Plan of Action reflects the international community's awareness of the importance of population trends for socio-economic development, and the socio-economic nature of the recommendations contained in this Plan of Action reflects its awareness of the crucial role that development plays in affecting population trends.[40]

Significantly, the final plan asserts that government subsidization of family planning services is both legitimate and necessary. The use of contraceptive devices has been the main way in which population size has been controlled, and, given the religious and moral opposition to forced sterilization and abortion, it will continue to be so in the foreseeable future. The dissemination of contraceptive information was approved by the Bucharest conference. Of course, widespread use of contraceptive devices has reduced population growth in the developed world. Now, sixty-five developing nations have introduced family control programs. The People's Republic of China has an advanced program which encourages late marriages and small families. As might be imagined, contraceptive services are readily available. Other nations that have instituted vigorous programs are Colombia, Costa Rica, Egypt, El Salvador, Hong Kong, Indonesia, Pakistan, Panama, the Philippines, Singapore, South Korea, Thailand, and Tunisia.[41]

Not only are nations doing something about population growth; they are addressing the problem of food availability. In the last twenty years, developing countries have increased their food production at about the same rate as developed countries.[42] Of course, developing countries have not achieved the agricultural riches of many Western nations (the United States, Canada, Australia, for example). Nevertheless, developing nations have increased their food production by an annual rate of 0.4% despite the fact that their populations have grown faster than those of developed countries. Food supplies in developing countries have also been bolstered by imports paid for by such raw materials as petroleum, copper, bauxite, and tin.[43] A brighter future is promised because high-yield varieties of wheat and rice have produced a continuing green revolution.

Concluding Remarks

Population problems will persist in the foreseeable future. The population of the world will double sometime before the middle of the twenty-first century. (Intentionally, I have made this projection extremely conservative. Most demographers predict that the population will double in considerably less time. My estimate is conservative because predictions rarely consider unusual factors. In this case, the effect of population control programs may be more dramatic than is generally believed.) The green revolution seems to assure that the world can handle this number of people. Eventually, population must be controlled or the person-land ratio will be more than the environment can tolerate. Since the ability of the land to absorb people depends on technological development, it cannot be predicted when the situation will become critical. Nevertheless, there are reasons to believe that dangers will be averted before land saturation takes place.

W. D. Borrie concludes his discussion of the population problem by observing that the leaders of society have accomplished so much in controlling disease, producing more food, extending life expectancy, and reducing the death rate that it is likely that means will be found to control population growth and to deal with future shortages of food.[44] No one can be sure that this optimistic prediction will be fulfilled, but there are no environmental, technological, or political reasons that assure that it will not. Therefore, solving the problems created by population growth depends on the will and ingenuity of humankind.

11. Pollution Problems

For many years, people assumed that the physical environment was static. It was believed that it could receive wastes and transform them, and, in general, be used as human beings saw fit without being affected. This conception of the biosphere was incorrect, but it was harmless as long as human activities were carried out on a relatively small scale. As human populations, and hence human activity, grew and as industrial and technological activity increased, the effects on the biosphere could no longer be ignored. In short, the pollution problem is real, and, since general awareness of it has developed relatively recently, its consequences are uncertain. That damage has been done is certain; the extent of damage is unknown; the ability of the physical environment and life systems to withstand more damage is uncertain. On the basis of evidence, panic is not justified; research and remedial measures are.

Assessing the actual potential damage of pollution is difficult because of lack of acceptable research techniques and because of the different claims made by a variety of interest groups.

Many conservationists seek to preserve natural settings because they prefer this type of environment. Their action is sustained by a value judgment that is not made by others. For example, many urban dwellers prefer the human-made environment of shops, restaurants, theaters, and concert halls. Both conservationists and urbanites judge on the basis of "amenities." It is fairly clear that there is no agreement as to what constitute real amenities, and consequently viewpoints supported by reference to amenities ought to be ignored.

Others predict disasters like a forthcoming ice age, a Noah-type flood from a rapid melting of ice masses in the North and South, the destruction of the atmosphere so that life-sustaining oxygen is used up, or a cataclysmic reordering of the balance of life. Although some of these possibilities are genuine, most of them are remote and are not supported by available evidence. The reasoning of such claimants is often an exercise in science fiction. Throughout history, fear has blocked great progress, and those who, out of fear, have stood in its way have been wrong more often than they have been right. One need only consider the conflict between religion and the advocates of Copernicus to recognize this general rule.

On the other hand, rationality requires that the more dangerous the consequences of action, the more cautious one's actions ought to be. Thus, although the cataclysmic consequences of pollution are remote, they should not be ignored. Caution is opposed by an interest group, industrialists, who view the problem with blinders (just as other special interest groups do). Industrialists are aware of the advantages of the industrial way of life. They also recognize the uncertainty of the dangers of pollution, yet they brush aside the consequences of their acts. It seems to me that it is rigidly rationalistic to suggest that aerosol sprays should continue to be produced because they have not been proved to damage the environment conclusively. The contribution that aerosol sprays make to human life is not sufficient to put aside remote cataclysmic possibilities.

Returning to the other side of the argument (so that the complexity of the problem be recognized), environmentalists, who seek to ban the manufacture of fertilizers and pesticides until they are proved safe, ignore the problem of the malnourished masses of people. Once again, balancing interests, a rational person would rather feed the millions of hungry than worry about the long-range health consequences to the present and future generations.

Other interests are involved, but these should give the reader an idea of the complexity of the problem. I suggest that the pollution problem requires an estimation of the immediacy of the danger, the magnitude of the danger, and the cost of remedying the situation. Some situations are worse than others; there is little evidence that the environment has been or will be destroyed in the near future. Remedial action is being taken more slowly than is desirable, but remedial action is being taken. And considerably more research must be done.

The Meaning of Pollution

Pollution is defined as the introduction of waste matter and/or surplus energy by human beings into the physical environment, which causes damage to persons, other living beings, and/or the environment. The damage may be done directly or indirectly. It may be acute or chronic, local or global. Pollution can be intense (high-level) or subtle (low-level). The negative effect may persist for a long period of time and, hence, may accumulate. If this is the case, a pollutant will produce chronic damage, and the damage may worsen as more of the pollutant is released into the atmosphere. Low-level, chronic pollution may be the most insidious danger because it is difficult to detect.

Acute, high-level pollution is considerably more dramatic and receives greater attention from the public, the news media, and law makers. Oil spills are an example of this kind of pollution. Although it would be foolish to minimize the danger of such accidents, it is unlikely that marine life, human health, or the ecosphere will be transformed by such events. The damage is local and short-range, and the environment will most likely recover.

The waste matter and surplus energy that constitute pollution are gases, particulate matter, liquids, solids, heat, and radiation. Waste matter becomes pollution when it is introduced into and does damage to the environment. It can be introduced at one place and transmitted through media such as air or water to other places. Pollution is discharged into the atmosphere, fresh waters, groundwaters, estuaries, and seas and onto the land. It damages the atmosphere, soil, bodies of waters, plants, non-human and human living things. Organisms can be destroyed or changed by the action of pollution. Relationships among communities and ecosystems can be transformed. In the long run, the ecosphere can be deleteriously affected.

Reiterating this important point, pollution can affect members of a particular species, a whole species (possibly causing it to disappear), or biological life as a whole. The wider the effect, the more likely that it has been caused by chronic pollution that has accumulated for years and has been transmitted by a number of media.

Climatic Effects of Pollution

The following factors adversely influence world climate: carbon dioxide (CO_2), sulfur dioxide (SO_2), particulate matter such as aerosols, the emissions of substances from vehicles and supersonic jet planes such as the Concorde, and the release of heat by combustion. Fuel combustion has increased the amount of CO_2 in the atmosphere in the last 120 years. Furthermore, as the burning of fossil fuels has increased, the amount of CO_2 in the atmosphere has increased.[1] It is thought that humans might increase the amount of CO_2 released into the atmosphere by 20% in the year 2000 and by a factor of 4 or more in the next century if current rates of consumption continue.[2] The danger of emitting too much CO_2 into the atmosphere is that a so-called greenhouse effect might take place. That is, the temperature of the planet may rise in much the same way as the temperature rises in a greenhouse. It is generally admitted that large urban centers become heat islands that cause shifts in the velocity, updraft, pattern, and turbulence of the wind.[3] Although some commentators predict that the temperature of the whole planet will rise, there is no direct evidence that this is occurring. Still, this is one of the remote possibilities whose consequences are frightening. If there is a significant greenhouse effect on a worldwide level, there may be an abrupt melting of the ice caps in the polar regions, which would cause worldwide flooding of catastrophic proportions. However, the actual thermodynamics of the atmosphere are exceedingly complex, involving the interaction of numerous forces, including some that counteract the greenhouse effect. In general, then, more research should be done before conclusions such as this inform action.

Sulfur dioxide is generally not thought to be a threat on a global scale. It causes local problems. In industrial areas, SO_2 emissions combined with smoke are believed to increase the death rate among those who have emphysema or bronchitis.[4] Most people are familiar with the incidences in English cities when human morality increased appreciably during the winter months because of pollution. As London reduced the amount of particulate matter in the air, which previously combined with SO_2, there were more hours of sunshine per day and a decrease in the incidence of death related to bronchitis and emphysema.[5]

Particulate matter exists naturally in the atmosphere. Human activity, industrial activity, the production of domestic smoke, and induced photochemical reactions involving trace gases such as SO_2 hydrocarbons add to the natural accumulation. Particulates act as nuclei which condense water vapor. As such, clouds are formed. The amount of rainfall is determined by the number of nuclei in the initial cloud-forming updraft. The addition of human-made particulates to the atmosphere increases cloudiness and may influence precipitation. Possibly of greater consequence, there has been a decrease in the amount of solar radiation over the past thirty or forty years, which has lowered surface temperatures.[6] The worst imagined consequence of such activity is that an ice age will be induced. This potential hazard is purely speculative.

It should be noted that "ice age" hypothesizing directly contradicts the claim of other speculators that the emission of SO_2 in the atmosphere will produce cataclysmic flooding through the greenhouse effect. The reason why these theories are doubted by many scientists is that each prediction is made by considering one factor and ignoring or minimizing the influence of other factors. These catalysts may cancel out the effect that each catalyst, alone, might produce. There might be unanticipated consequences. There also are other natural and induced environmental factors which bear on the climatic future.

Jet flights, especially the introduction of supersonic transports (SSTs) to the skies, have produced the fear that their emissions will transform the stratosphere. It is thought that SST emissions could reduce the amount of stratospheric ozone through photochemical oxidation. If this were so, then living beings would be exposed to harmful doses of ultraviolet radiation. As of now, scientists believe that the amount of contaminants introduced into the stratosphere by SSTs will fall within the range of natural global variation.[7]

Heat caused by combustion, which is found extensively in urban-industrial areas, potentially influences climate. The most obvious manifestation of this pollutant is the creation of heat islands in large cities. It is recognized that heat combustion increases cloudiness, but it is thought that the effects are primarily local. Dramatic increases in power generation requirements might create escalating demands for water resources to cool down equipment. This might lead to water loss by water evaporation and to traumatic changes in aquatic conditions. These deleterious consequences are expected to be local rather than global.[8]

In summary, the evidence suggests that most of the devastating global possibilities are remote. There are definite negative local effects of pollution on climate. Such changes affect the environment (reduce the amount of water and interfere with photosynthesis). These consequences are generally local and acute. Whenever industry cleans its tools, salubrious reversals are noted.

Ecological Effects of Pollution

Radioactivity from nuclear power as a source of pollution receives great attention. The position of nuclear power in the public mind is similar to that of airplanes in the first half of this century. Just as the drama and danger of air travel both attracted and frightened humankind, the cataclysmic power of nuclear explosions is both awesome and terrifying today. People are mesmerized by its power and potential for service and horrified by the prospect of a nuclear accident. And just as air travel became safer as the air industry sought to assuage the fears of its clientele, peaceful nuclear use is more intensively checked for radioactive pollution than any other potential form of pollution. This monitoring is especially intensive around industrial sites where nuclear power is used and nuclear wastes are disposed. Proponents of nuclear energy assert that not much background radiation has been added to the environment and there is little reason to believe that any added radiation produces somatic or genetic damage.[9] Aside from nuclear explosions and reactor accidents, wastes from nuclear power production and fuel processing seem to have no appreciable global effects. Studies indicate that the risks of reactor accidents are remarkably small.[10] This can be claimed even after the Three Mile Island incident. Nuclear reactors provide only a small fraction of the total exposure to radiation compared with doses from natural (cosmic), medical (x-rays), occupational, and military sources.

These views are challenged by many commentators (such as Barry Commoner). The counterargument is based primarily on the sheer devastating potential of nuclear accidents and nuclear misuse. As I have argued earlier, fear is justified. When radioactivity is released into the atmosphere, it perseveres. The more that is produced, the greater are the chances of an accident occurring. Major accidents, especially if they became commonplace, would have serious effects on organisms. The released radiation would eventually contaminate human beings as they are transmitted through the food chain. Ultimately, somatic and genetic changes could take place.

As can be deduced, the problem of nuclear waste storage is extremely important. The more that is stored, the greater the chance of an accident. It cannot be denied that great effort is being made to develop safeguards against accidents and that new means of safe storage are being sought. Many nations are investigating the possibility of storing nuclear wastes in insoluble refractive blocks and of developing fast breeder reactors, which would produce less waste because they make more efficient use of fuel.[11]

Overall, the empirical data indicate that industrial producers are acting carefully. Fear springs from the evidence of history that human beings eventually abuse nature and rationalize their misdeeds. This tendency intensifies when a system becomes socially and economically entrenched. Cigarette manufacturers deny the uncontrovertible conclusions of research that have been verified many times over. The power of industry is so great that it can mobilize experts and public officials to counteract the data of science. The nuclear industry may exhibit similar tendencies if the populace and government begin to feel secure about the safety of nuclear use. Eventually, carelessness may creep into industrial practice, and hosts of industrial fellow-travelers will conspire to mask the evidence of mistakes, to discredit critics, and to threaten the populace with loss of service and higher prices if they are forced to make amends.

I find this argument so convincing that I cannot endorse nuclear power. Since, in reality, the move toward a greater use of nuclear power seems irresistible, I believe that pressure should be exerted to slow the development of nuclear power so that safety measures stay several steps ahead of nuclear development. This would be costly but would have to be tolerated because of the grave consequences of nuclear accidents. Industry, in its resolute, single-minded pursuit of profit, invariably ignores dangers until it is forced by external criticism to recognize them. This means that safety measures are ordinarily after the fact and *remedial*. In this context, *prevention* is required.

Pesticides seem to be both a boon to humankind and an ecological threat. Organochlorine pesticides such as DDT and its derivatives protect crops and increase yields. In a period of population growth, this has to be viewed as a positive factor, and it is usually viewed as such in developing countries where population growth is extreme. On the other hand, organochlorines tend to persist in the environment and are possible threats to living beings. The evidence indicates that most organochlorines are concentrated in the tissues of animals and humans. Already, the concentration of low-level pollution in coastal and estuarine areas is higher than desirable and may cause damage. Residues of organochlorines in fish are associated with the disappearance of some fish-eating birds. Reproductive inhibition or failure in some species of fish and crustaceans has been reported in seawater. Some plankton species may have failed to survive because of low-level organochlorine pollution.[12]

As developed countries have curtailed the use of DDT, acute pollution has declined. Carbamate and organophosphate pesticides are being used as substitutes because they are less persistent than organochlorines and are nonaccumulative.[13] It may be concluded that the use of pesticides can be dangerous and should be carefully monitored. Developing countries, which always face mass starvation, do not have the luxury of choice. They must use pesticides in order to increase their food supplies.

The natural food craze which is popular in wealthy nations such as the United States seems to be in part a consequence of scare tactics. There is little evidence that human beings are suffering acute damage from the use of pesticides.[14] The dangers are remote. In order to make a sound judgment, it is necessary to balance the advantages of the use of pesticides with its dangers. Currently, reason favors the continuing use of pesticides and continuing research to investigate potential dangers and to seek substitutes for the more dangerous pesticides.

I consider the case of pesticides to be quite different from that of nuclear power. In the latter instance, alternative sources of energy are available. Some are presently feasible such as liquid coal; others are in the development stage such as solar energy. At the same time, fossil fuels have not been exhausted. Consequently, there is time to develop nuclear power gradually (if at all). On the other hand, millions of people are starving. Consequently, food production must be increased. Society should gamble on there being no long-term devastating consequences of using pesticides but continue research on its side effects. If evidence shows permanent damage, then the use of pesticides ought to be curtailed.

Trace metals, produced through industrial use, such as mercury and lead, are possibly global pollutants. Acute mercury poisoning can be fatal or can cause permanent damage to the central nervous system. It has been estimated that human food should not contain more than 0.5 parts per million (ppm) of mercury and such nations as the United States forbid any residue of mercury in human food. Electrical industries, industrial catalytic processes, paper manufacturers, and chloralkal plants are the primary sources of mercury. The mercury that is introduced into the atmosphere quickly finds its way into oceans and inland waters. Low levels of mercury can inhibit photosynthesis in some species of plankton and can alter fish behavior. It is thought that marine organisms can tolerate more than 1.0 ppm of mercury. This amount can affect human health, especially in countries such as Japan, where the diet relies heavily on seafood. So far, the evidence does not indicate that human health has been deleteriously affected from present levels of mercury in food in countries whose diets do not heavily rely on fish.[15]

One of the dangers of mercury is that it persists in the sea for long periods of time. Consequently, there has been an attempt to monitor carefully the amount of mercury that is released into the atmosphere. Improvements are being made in controlling industrial uses of mercury.

Lead consumption is rising throughout the world, and consequently so is the amount being emitted into the atmosphere. Lead is both toxic and persistent. High levels of lead in the blood can produce mental abnormality in children. But this condition is produced primarily in children who chew objects coated with lead-containing paint. In more insidious ways, lead is introduced into the blood system. Some is inhaled from automobile exhaust systems; some is ingested in food that contains lead residues; and some is taken in water that has been contaminated by fallout, industrial discharges, and natural erosion.[16] The major source of the lead in the environment is petroleum. Many nations, including the United States, have taken measures to control the amount of lead in gasoline.

Other metals—cadmium, nickel, chromium, zinc, and arsenic—have been found in the atmosphere and in rivers, oceans, and organisms.[17]

Whether organisms have the capacity to tolerate low levels of these metals is not fully known, but dangerous levels have been registered. It is necessary to control the amounts of metals released in the environment. Effort is being expended in this direction, but more will have to be done. Once again, technological innovation is the remedy for this form of pollution.

Nutrients introduced into marine environments by the use of fertilizers and detergents and by waste disposal cause eutrophication. This is a process of enrichment that leads to dominance by simpler forms of life (bluegreen algae, for example) in aquatic ecosystems, thereby forcing out free-living fish and other animals. These alterations take place because light penetration for photosynthesis is reduced, oxygen is depleted, and the dominant organisms produce toxins that inhibit the growth and survival of more desirable species. The problem is global because 90% of fish species reside, pass through, or breed in estuaries and coastal areas, which are primary sites of nutrient pollution.[18] As of now, it is both technically and economically difficult to control nutrient discharges. Nevertheless, it is essential to devise measures for reducing eutrophication, especially since the sea is potentially a great source of food.

Oil spills from tankers are dramatic examples of damage done to the environment by industry. The consequences are obvious and immediate. Marine plants and animals are poisoned; plankton may be adversely affected. Seabirds may be prevented from flying and may even be asphyxiated or poisoned. Carcinogenic substances may enter the food chain, although this is considered unlikely because only a small amount of oil is introduced into human food in this way. There is not yet much evidence to substantiate the claim that ocean resources are being damaged significantly for extended periods of time by oil pollution. Nevertheless, oil production is increasing, so danger exists. Fortunately, the loss of amenity together with the immediacy of damage has led to measures to control oil spills.

The most obvious conclusions that can be drawn about the pollution of the environment are that it is increasing and it poses a threat to the ecosphere, human health, and the seas. Persistent metals, industrial chemicals, and persistent pesticides are the most important pollutants.[19] Eutrophication is another process that adversely affects water quality and the ability of marine organisms to survive. Gaseous and particulate air pollution may produce long-term effects on human and plant health. The use of nuclear energy requires constant surveillance because of the overwhelming potential for destruction.

Conclusion

For some time society has been aware of the dramatic effects of acute pollution. The atmosphere of mining towns and putrefaction from oil spills exemplify this kind of pollution. Now, the insidious consequences of pollutants that gradually accumulate and persist over time pose a much greater threat to the world. Without research, people would not become aware of the danger until remedial action could no longer be effective.

Two reactions to the pollution problem are typical. Industrial spokesmen, relying on the fact that the extent and potential damage of chronic, low-level pollution are uncertain, seek to avoid restrictions on pollutants until empirical evidence conclusively resolves uncertainties. They argue that it is too expensive to restrict production simply because there is potential danger. Some no-growth futurists and environmentalists seek to restrict industrial practices wherever pollution problems exist until conclusive evidence is found and/or adequate pollution controls are developed. Some, such as E. J. Mishan, blame many of society's current problems on the automobile, and suggest a massive restructuring of the social landscape.

Both responses strike me as being unwise. The former ignores danger until it is too late; the latter cavalierly brushes aside economic and social realities and disregards real human needs. Making pollution control the *first* social priority would result in massive economic depression and would lead to the starvation of millions of people.

A rational approach to the problem is to weigh the advantages of each industrial and agricultural process that pollutes the environment against the potential threat. At the same time, the evidence indicting a process as a pollutant should be evaluated. For example, the radiation from nuclear processes has not been shown to be a major pollutant. Nevertheless it ought to be monitored with exceeding care because of its inherent power to damage the ecosphere and human health. Since the potential damage of SSTs is uncertain and the evidence suggests that little pollution is discharged into the atmosphere, the use of SSTs ought not to be restricted, but their effect on the environment should continue to be studied.

Eutrophication definitely changes the marine environment and reduces the diversity of free-living fish. Because fish are needed to feed growing populations and because other forms of food from the sea may also be threatened, eutrophication that is caused by human activity ought to be controlled. We can only speculate about the long-range dangers of upsetting aquatic ecosystems, but because it has been demonstrated that food supplies are destroyed by eutrophication, these dangers should be taken seriously. Together, these considerations should override the arguments of industrial interests that it is too costly to control eutrophication now.

The actions of the automotive industry demonstrate how rational solutions to real problems are eschewed. The automobile is a pollutant whose effects are uncertain. Nevertheless, there is more than a remote possibility that human health is impaired by the inhalation of emissions from vehicular exhausts. Automobiles use up an excessive amount of petroleum, thereby contributing greatly to the energy crisis. Congestion also reduces the amenities of urban living. These factors suggest that policies concerning automobile usage should change. Safety standards should be enforced despite the protests of the automotive industry; public transportation (electric buses, trains) should be revived; and alternative clean forms of automotive power ought to be studied and subsidized. It is sad to relate that the famed Stanley Steamer, which failed because Henry Ford put his energy behind the combustion engine, was a clean, efficient source of automotive power. It is a tragedy of capitalistic politics that the automotive industry in the United States has used its political power to subvert public transportation systems.

A mistake that may prove to be tragic in the future is that the American government continues to subsidize air travel and to neglect train travel. Although jet transportation has not yet been shown to create a significant health or climatic hazard, the possibility remains that it does. Furthermore, as the public makes greater use of the airlines, the potential for danger in the future will increase. Concentrating all effort in a limited number of directions is politically, economically, and ecologically unwise. The increased use of petroleum and petroleum products by the United States should have convinced American political and social leaders of this reality. Nevertheless, the United States continues to support automotive and air travel to the exclusion of other forms of transportation. It puts off the enforcement of reasonable safety and energy-saving standards and it refuses to invest in research on alternative kinds of transportation. Future crises may bring about new approaches to meeting transportation needs, but the opportunity to adopt them voluntarily is being lost.

In my recommendations, I have attempted to incorporate a rational approach to pollution control. It is foolish to rush into remedial action when dangers are remote. It is equally foolish to ignore remote dangers. There is no evidence that pollution is so extensive as to be irreversible.

Nevertheless, no-growth futurists rightly claim that unencumbered industrial development might make our planet uninhabitable. The case of transportation demonstrates that people are not dealing directly or rationally with pollution. Something is being done, but hesitantly and halfheartedly.

To put the problem into perspective it can be said that enough is being done about pollution that the greatest threat to the future of humankind is still a worldwide nuclear war. Pollution control should be stepped up, but it cannot be pursued so aggressively that the needs of millions of people who live at or below the subsistence level are ignored.

12. Conclusion: A Rational Future

In writing this book, I have set two main goals: first, to show that industrial society is not a social relic as no-growth futurists maintain, and, second, that liberalism remains a living political tool by which contemporary moral needs can be met. It has been argued that an essential liberalism could be devised which promotes material development as a necessary means to self-development (self-development being the necessary goal of liberal morality) and that liberal government (a representative system that incorporates protection against excessive government authority and provides fundamental freedoms) is an efficient vehicle through which self-development can be realized.

Nations that are structured along liberal lines, such as the Western democracies, have a moral obligation to promote greater economic equity within their boundaries so that the socially and politically disadvantaged can improve themselves. No nation has achieved an equitable distribution of social opportunity. In all likelihood, this remains an unrealizable ideal. Nevertheless, much greater equity can be established, and liberal society must dedicate itself to this end. In order to provide greater opportunity for the disadvantaged, it is necessary that industrial growth continue.

Expansion cannot take the path recommended by conservative theorists; that is the economic and social future cannot be determined by a free market. Conservative social policy is ineffective because Smith's "invisible hand" is a chimera. The market cannot be free because industrial interests are too powerful to permit competition; the government cannot be trusted to establish open competition because it would be bought off by large industries. The inevitable result of attempting to reinstitute a free market would be the establishment of an economic tyranny. Furthermore, industrialists would be so mesmerized by the prospects of greater profits that they would not institute adequate environmental protection from pollution. As this is being written, the automotive industry in the United States is renewing efforts to obtain a reduction in pollution restrictions in the hope of competing effectively with the Japanese automotive industry. The need for pollution control is genuine, and conservative theorists are blind to it.

The rational approach to industrial expansion requires that government influence the path taken by industry. Government should require that businesses operate in such a way that scarce resources are conserved and problems such as pollution are overcome. In order for government to promote the general welfare, liberals must first convince the public of the need to modify industrial growth in order to protect and improve the environment. Liberals can achieve this end only if they abandon the shrill cries of revolutionaries and the exaggerated claims of political extremists and clearly place their programs within the context of American political theory and history.

Many liberals have developed an aversion to patriotism because the nationalism associated with it, especially since the experience of Hitler and the failure of the U.S. government to voluntarily provide civil rights for blacks and other minorities, seems reprehensible. Although the kind of patriotism that leads to irrational nationalism and that conceals social injustice ought to be condemned, it should be publicly proclaimed that the American political system is an application of liberal morality. When the continuity that exists between liberal policy recommendations and the Constitution and American history is clarified, the liberal message will not be abrasive to politically neutral Americans.

Besides seeking to make industrial growth fulfill genuine social needs, liberals should try to enact laws and establish social policies that distribute wealth and economic opportunity to the advantage of the poor. I am not calling for an equal distribution of wealth, but an equitable one. The poor should obtain greater rewards for their services, and acquire greater social and economic mobility through increased educational and job opportunities. Furthermore, tax laws should be restructured so that the special advantages that permit the excessive accumulation of unused private wealth and that favor those who make a large amount of money are withdrawn.

Although most of the methods I have suggested here apply to the unique situation in this country, comparable legislation can be recommended for other liberal nations.

In summary, liberal policy for liberal nations and for the first world should be to sustain economic growth and material development by directing industrial development along desirable lines. At the same time, remedial legislation should be enacted to rectify the maldistribution of economic advantages. It is most important that the poor obtain greater opportunity for self-development. Possibly the great mistake of remedial social programs today is that they overemphasize supplying goods and money to the poor. Although such action may be necessary for immediate survival, self-development programs are long-range solutions.

Regarding the communist world, I have argued that the communist political system is morally inferior to the liberal political system because it operates on authoritarian principles. In making this judgment, I consciously reject a prevailing ethical relativity. Authoritarian political systems are undesirable because ultimately they give rise to self-interested, irrational governments; that is, they create tyrannies. This is inevitable because people are fundamentally selfish and irrational when pursuing their perceived interests. In an authoritarian state, the irrational, selfish tendencies of leaders flourish. There are no legislative or political checks on them. One of the reasons why King Lear is led to a disastrous division of his kingdom is that the years in which he ruled absolutely dulled his senses so that he heard only flattery. History, too, demonstrates that authoritarian political systems eventually become corrupt.

Even though Western liberal democracies may be morally superior to communist nations, liberals can have little direct or immediate effect on the communist world. Military power is too highly developed for war to be waged; the large communist nations (the USSR and the People's Republic of China) are too well-established for revolutions to be induced from outside. However, liberals can *advertise* the virtues of their system so that people within these nations might follow liberal paths in the far distant future. A second liberal policy is to continue to seek peaceful solutions to world problems and to expand communication and trade with communist nations. This is not to suggest that aggressive action by communist nations, such as the invasion of Afghanistan by Russian troops, should be ignored or countenanced. Rather, liberals should not lose sight of the advantages of détente while taking measures to counteract hostile military actions.

One of the great moral challenges facing liberals and liberal nations concerns the plight of the third world. Developing nations have obtained considerable political power through the United Nations. They supply some key raw materials that are used by the developed and communist worlds. Despite these facts, developing nations are beset by innumerable internal problems. They suffer from overpopulation, hostile natural environments, and poverty. The political machinery in these nations are usually authoritarian; the gap between the rich and the poor is greatest there; their governments are highly unstable. Although these nations desire to fabricate their own resources, their people do not have the education and skills needed to take advantage of technology.

Given traditional liberal goals, it would seem that liberal nations should seek to establish Western-style democracies in the third world so that industrial development can take place there. This ought not to be done because liberal nations—administered by human beings inflicted with the common human defect, a selfish desire for power—would not promote the interests of the third world. They would do what the English did in India and Africa.

Instead of trying to convert the third world to liberalism through political or military action, liberal nations should seek to improve the economies of the third world, while tying the advantages given to these nations to internal policies which improve the living conditions of the poor. Third world nations should be given the opportunity to fabricate their own resources. However, the exportation of technology to the third world should be undertaken only as third world nations introduce population control measures and improve their educational systems. If measures such as these are taken, then third world governments will become more stable, which will increase the likelihood that the third world will voluntarily adopt liberal political systems.

Developments in transportation, communication, and industry in the last eighty years are bringing about the reality of a dependent *economic* world. However, there is little likelihood that one *political* world can be realized in the foreseeable future. People are too divided by social interest, language differences, and political style to desire one political world. Representatives of political, economic, and social groups have so much power that they will be able to prevent attempts to bring about one political world either through force or conversion.

A single political world can be realized only after a single social and economic world is established. The development of one social and economic world will have to be an evolutionary process that spans a considerable period of time. If such a state evolves—and there is no certainty that it will evolve—then politicians will devise a political system to organize the economic, social world and philosophers will rationalize and justify the political system.

Throughout this book, I have maintained that industrial development is the means by which the interests of the poor in the first world and the interests of all people in the third and communist worlds can be met. I have argued that technological innovation is the only means by which resource shortages can be overcome. Because of my commitment to technological growth, I oppose the contentions of no-growth futurists. Chapters 8 and 9 have been devoted to showing that industrialization has not run its course and that economic growth can continue.

There are several problems, however, that must be solved if a better world is to be produced. Pollution and population growth ought to be controlled. I have argued that the dangers are not so acute as no-growth futurists contend, but they are real. Although I have not emphasized this, it strikes me that the single greatest problem confronting human-kind is the possibility of irrational political action leading to a nuclear confrontation. The desirability of avoiding nuclear war is another reason for recommending political détente.

In conclusion, I do not contend that industrial growth will continue and that economic, social, and political problems will be overcome. I maintain that there are no environmental, social, or political realities that rule out continuing improvement. Stated positively, the conditions for salubrious growth are present. Human choice will determine the future.

Notes

Notes to Chapter 1

1. Donella & Dennis Meadows, Jorgen Randers, William Behrens, *The Limits of Growth*, New York: Signet Books, 1972.
Jay Forrester, *World Dynamics*, Cambridge, MA: Wright-Allen Press, 1971.
Mihajlo Mesarovich and Eduard Pestel, *Mankind at the Turning Point*, New York: Dutton & Co., 1974.

2. Raymond Vernon, "An Interpretation of the Oil Crisis," *The Oil Crisis*, edited by R. Vernon, New York: W. W. Norton and Co., 1976, p. 14.

3. Meadows, Ranfers, *et. al.*, op. ci., p. 33.

4. Dennis L. Meadows & Donella L. Meadows, *Toward Global Equilibrium*, Cambridge, MA: Wright-Allen Press, Inc., 1973. See Forrester, "Counter-intuitive Behavior of Social Systems," pp. 14-18.

5. Meadows, Randers, *et al.*, op. cit., pp. 48-50.

6. Forrester, op. cit., p. 27.

7. Barry Commoner, *The Poverty of Power: Energy and the Economic Crisis*, New York: Alfred A. Knopf, 1976, pp. 90-91.

8. Meadows, Randers, *et al.*, op. cit., p. 71.

9. Ibid., p. 69.

10. In a survey conducted by the Institute of Situational Ethics, a majority of those interviewed indicated that the national speed limit should be raised to 73 MPH despite their knowledge that lower speed limits save lives.

11. Today this claim could no longer be made. People have lost confidence in technology as a consequence of constant inflation, recurring depression, and persistent no-growth propagandizing. Nevertheless, it could still be argued that steady-state planning has not been forthcoming.

12. Marion Brienes, "Smog Comes to Los Angeles," *Southern California Quarterly*, Volume LVIII, Number 4 (Winter 1976), p. 515.

13. Barry Commoner, *The Closing Circle: Nature, Man, and Technology*, New York: Alfred A. Knopf, 1971, pp. 67-68.

14. Ibid., p. 69.

15. Ibid., p. 76.

16. Jorgen Randers and Donella H. Meadows, "The Carrying Capacity of Our Global Environment: A Look at Ethical Alternatives," *Toward Global Equilibrium*, edited by Meadows & Meadows, pp. 319-320.

17. Nigel Calder, "Head South with All Deliberate Speed," *Smithsonian*, Vol. 8, No. 10 (January, 1978), p. 39.

18. Commoner, *The Closing Circle*, op. cit., p. 96.

19. Ibid., pp. 103-104. See also, Jay Martin Anderson, "The Eutrophication of Lakes," *Toward Global Equilibrium*, edited by Meadows & Meadows, pp. 119-120, pp. 132-133, pp. 137-138.

20. Commoner, *The Closing Circle*, op. cit., p. 105.

21. Ibid., pp. 222-223.

22. Ibid., pp. 223-224.

23. Jorgen Randers, "DDT Movement in the Global Environment," *Toward Global Equilibrium*, edited by Meadows & Meadows, op. cit., pp. 73-75.

24. Alison A. Anderson and Jay Martin Anderson, "System Simulation to Identify Environmental Research Needs: Mercury Contamination," *Toward Global Equilibrium*, edited by Meadows & Meadows, op. cit., pp. 101-102.

25. Meadows, Randers, *et al.*, op. cit., p. 41.

26. Ibid., p. 57.

27. Ibid., pp. 119-134, p. 148.

28. Ibid., p. 58.

29. Ibid., p. 58.

30. Commoner, *The Closing Circle*, op. cit., p. 149.

31. Ibid., p. 148.

32. Meadows, Randers, *et al.*, op. cit., p. 62.

33. Ibid., p. 154.

34. E. J. Mishan, *The Costs of Economic Growth*, New York: Praeger Publications, 1971, pp. 109-121.

35. Hazel Henderson, "Ecologists versus Economists," *Harvard Business Review*, July-August 1973, p. 34.

36. Ibid., p. 34.

37. Kenneth E. Boulding, *The Economy of Love and Fear*, Belmont, CA: Wadsworth Publishing Co., 1973.

38. Meadows, Randers, *et al.*, op. cit., pp. 169-171. More general but compatible suggestions are made in the second Club of Rome study. See Mihajlo Mesorovich and Eduard Pestel, *Mankind at the Turning Point*, op. cit., pp. 143-149.

39. Randers and Meadows, "The Carrying Capacity of Our Global Environment," op. cit., p. 333.

40. Ibid., p. 335.

Notes to Chapter 2

1. Ralph N. Clough, A. Doak Barnett, Morton H. Halperin, Jerome H. Kahan, *The United States, China, and Arms Control*, Washington, D.C.: The Brookings Institution, 1975, p. 9.

2. Brian Crozier, *The Future of Communist Power*, London: Eyre & Spottiswoode, 1970, pp. 28-29.

3. William Ebenstein and Edwin Fogelman, *Today's ISMS*, Englewood Cliffs, New Jersey: Prentice-Hall, Inc., 1980, pp. 75-77.

4. Crozier, op. cit., p. 32.

5. Ibid., p. 33.
6. Ibid., p. 63.
7. Clough, *et al.*, op. cit., p. 7.
8. Ibid., p. 8.
9. Ibid., p. 11.
10. Ebenstein and Fogelman, op. cit., p. 34.
11. Ebenstein and Fogelman, op. cit., p. 32-35.
12. Ibid., p. 36.
13. Ibid., p. 99.
14. This tendency is apparent in American legislation that requires industrial and automotive pollution controls, standards for disposal of industrial wastes, etc. It is true that environmentalists express dissatisfaction with the timidity of these measures, but industrialists also complain because production is hampered.
15. *The New York Times*, September 19, 1979, p. 1.
16. Energy sources that can substitute for oil—coal, coal converted to liquid form, and shale oil—increase environmental hazards. Coal conversion is linked with the development of strip mining which devastates an area. Furthermore, coal conversion, as well as shale-oil production, depletes water supplies. Coal conversion, also, increases the danger of cancer. In a West Virginia plant where this process is employed, there has been a 16-37 times greater incidence of verified and probable skin cancer. (R. J. Sexton, "The Hazards to Health in the Hydrogenation of Coal," *Archives of Environmental Health*, Vol. 1, 1960.) Coal burning releases sulfur dioxide in the air which interferes with the lung's ability to reduce the effects of dust and other pollutants. Industry, as might be expected, has fought attempts to use devices to get rid of sulfur dioxide.

The main difficulty with increasing the use of these energy alternatives is that the cost of production is greater than the cost of oil. The Ford administration sought to set a floor on oil prices, so that the production of alternative sources would be encouraged. (A Kissinger statement made in a Paris meeting of oil-consumer countries, *New York Times*, March 21, 1975.)

For fuller discussion of this topic see Commoner, *The Poverty of Power*, New York: Alfred A. Knopf, 1976, Ch. 4, pp. 66-81.

17. As is generally known, the problems of India are great. Herman Kahn maintains that India, with a population of 600 million, creates one-half of the world's food problems. At the same time, there is an inadequate governmental expenditure on agriculture, especially the development of irrigation facilities and fertilizer production. (Herman Kahn, *The Next 200 Years*, New York: William Morrow and Co., Inc., 1976, pp. 136-138.)

Meadows, *et al.*, note that food production in the developing countries is barely holding constant, while it is growing in the developed countries. (Meadows, *The Limits of Growth*, op. cit., p. 58.)

Some of these conditions have improved. Developing countries have begun to deal with population problems. India has altered national priorities so that agricultural growth has begun. These glimmerings of hope will be discussed fully later.

18. "Housing: It's Outasight," *Time Magazine*, September 12, 1977, pp. 50-57.
19. Ibid.
20. Although oil companies applauded President Carter's energy proposals insofar as they sought higher prices, oil spokesmen (H. J. Haynes, chairman of the Standard Oil Co. of California and Colin Lee, a planner for Continental Oil Company) objected to the absence of incentives for the exploration and development of additional oil and natural gas supplies. (*New York Times*, April 22, 1977, p. 6.)
21. In 1969, there were fifty American counties with populations in excess of 50,000 people whose median family incomes ranged between $11,822 and $16,710. (*CBS News Almanac*, New Jersey: Hammond Almanac, Inc., 1977, p. 225.)
22. North America, for example, has approached a stable population. There the population increase for 1965-1974 was 1.0% compared with an average of 2.3% in Asia. This is a troublesome statistic because Asia already contains more than one-half of the world's population. Furthermore, Asia does not possess the agricultural potential of North America. (See *CBS News Almanac*, 1977, op. cit., p. 223.)
23. The nonliberal bigot also hates government. His reason is that government has promoted school busing and affirmative action programs which supposedly advance the cause of racial minorities at the expense of the white majority. The political conservative is anti-government because he believes that the government impedes natural economic development.

Notes to Chapter 3

1. T.H. Green is generally recognized as the transitional figure between the classic liberal position of passive government to the contemporary liberal position of positive government. H. J. Laski contends that Green was the philosophic inspiration for the "gains in legislation of the last fifty years." (Laski, *The Decline of Liberalism*, London: Oxford University Press, 1940, pp. 11-12.) For an extensive treatment of Green's influence, see: Melvin Richter, *The Politics of Conscience*, Cambridge, MA: Harvard University Press, 1964, pp. 267-291.
2. Statistics indicate that the share of U.S. personal wealth distribution has neither clearly increased not decreased in this century. (Stanley Lebergott, *The American Economy*, Princeton, N.J.: Princeton University Press, 1976, p. 162.)
    On the other hand, the concentration of wealth has increased. The top 1% of the top 200,000 wealthholders own 32% of all investment assets and 2% of individual stockholders own 66½% of all personally-owned stock. (Willard R. Johnson, "Should the Poor Buy No-Growth?", *Daedalus*, Fall 1973, p. 177.)
3. This is the classic trickle-down model of economic growth. The underlying theme is that growth of the GNP (Gross National Product) is the only means of helping the poor. It is noted that between 1959 and 1971, the people classified as poor by Census Bureau standards decreased 14.4 million or 1.2 million per year. (Johnson, op. cit., p. 169.)

4. My concept of selfishness is derived from Thomas Hobbes—the forerunner of classical liberalism. When I claim that human beings are fundamentally selfish, I mean that they pursue goals that are adopted because they are perceived to satisfy personal desires. I believe that all people start out this way. Psychological studies by James Piaget and Lawrence Kohlberg on the development of human values support my view. They claim that education and experiences can educate people to be less selfish. (See Richard Hersch, *Promoting Moral Growth: from Piaget to Kohlberg,* 1979.) For this reason, I will argue that human intelligence is the means by which human selfishness can be modified at the end of this chapter.

As I have indicated, a minority of people are capable of modifying personal selfishness so that they may act fairly with others. Nevertheless, nations have not reached sufficient maturity so that their policies are *predominantly* just. Most nations generally set goals that are narrowly conceived and benefit themselves economically, militarily, and politically. Probably, nations generally act selfishly because most people generally act selfishly. Of course, I do not imply that *any* nation *always* acts selfishly.

5. Vernon, "An Interpretation of the Oil Crisis," *The Oil Crisis,* edited by R. Vernon, New York: W. W. Norton & Co., 1976, p. 14.

6. Oil production in the United States declined after 1957. Oil company expenditures for exploration and development increased 200% between 1942 and 1957. After 1957, when the dependence on foreign oil began, expenditures fell 25% in the next ten years. The factor that led to this change was the cheapness of foreign oil relative to indigenous oil. Between 1942 and 1952, the price of oil increased by more than 100%; since 1957, it remained relatively constant. A report of the National Petroleum Council in July 1970 asserts that "none of the 11 regions has been adequately explored" and that potential oil reserves in the U.S. "may exceed 432 billion barrels." Barry Commoner maintains that the only variable that accounts for the decisions of the oil companies is the desire to make greater profits. (See Chapter 3, Barry Commoner, *The Poverty of Power,* New York: Alfred A. Knopf, 1976.)

7. Commoner, *The Poverty of Power,* op. cit., pp. 82-120.

8. Ibid., pp. 155-210.

9. According to government studies, 3.19 billion hectares of land are potentially arable. If coupled with rational policies, there should be sufficient food for some time. (See President's Science Advisory Panel on the World's Food Supply, *The World Food Problem,* Washington: U.S. Government Printing Office, 1967.)

It has been noted that India's food problem is partially a result of bad planning. Recently, India has shifted its interest from industrial to agricultural development. This produced a record grain crop in 1976. Such evidence suggests that the potential for better food production exists even in nations whose problems are most severe. This contradicts the findings of no-growth futurists. (*CBS News World Almanac,* 1977, op. cit., p. 545.)

10. Between 1950 and 1970, farm output increased 40%. Each farmer produced enough to feed fifteen people in 1950 and, in 1970, produced enough

food to feed forty-seven people. This increase was attained by replacing farm labor with machinery and by introducing the use of chemical fertilizers. (Commoner, *The Poverty of Power*, op. cit., p. 160, p. 170.)

Notes to Chapter 4

1. I do not imply by this last remark that liberalism rules out government action to promote racial integration. I do assert, however, that liberals must address the problem. This will entail showing (if it can be shown) that government-enforced racial integration is an exception to the liberal rule. And, government-enforced racial integration is not an ad hoc exception.

2. The French Revolution inspired the first burst of conservative philosophizing. Subsequently, conservatives found embryonic traces of their thought in the writings of Plato, Augustine, Thomas Aquinas, etc. Nevertheless, it is appropriate to date the founding of conservatism with the articulate opposition of Edmund Burke to the revolutionary ardor of the French.

The reason for claiming that conservatism is a reaction to liberalism is that the revolution in France was inspired by Locke's theory. As conservatism developed, it unequivocally opposed liberal reform. (Anthony Quinton, *The Politics of Imperfection*, London & Boston: Faber & Faber, 1978, p. 9.)

3. Ibid., p. 16.

4. Ibid., p. 17.

5. M. Morton Auerbach, *The Conservative Illusion*, New York: Columbia University Press, 1959, pp. 20-25.

6. Burke defined political society thusly:

> a partnership in all science . . . in all art . . . in every virtue. . . . It becomes a partnership between those who are living . . . those who are dead and those who are to be born. . . . It is but a clause according to a fixed compact . . . which hold all physical and moral natures each in their appointed place. . . . To this compact man must be obedient . . . for if he is not, Nature is disobeyed and the rebellious are . . . cast far . . . from this world of reason, order, peace, and virtue . . . into the antagonist world of madness, discord, vice, and confusion.

Ibid., p. 36.

7. Karl Marx, *A Contribution to the Critique of Political Economy*, second edition, translated by N. I. Stone, Chicago: Charles H. Kerr and Co., 1904, pp. 10-15.

8. Karl Marx, "The Coming Upheaval," excerpted from *The Poverty of Philosophy*, *The Marx-Engels Reader*, second edition, edited by Robert C. Tucker, New York: W. W. Norton & Company, 1978, pp. 218-219.

9. Marx took from Smith and Ricardo, the fathers of classical economic theory, theories of value and price. (Ernest Mandel, *An Introduction to Marxist Economic Theory*, New York: Pathfinder Press, 1973, pp. 13-17.)

10. Sidney Hook, *Reason, Social Myths and Democracy*, New York: Harper Torchbooks, 1966, pp. 137-139.

11. M. M. Knappen, *Constitutional and Legal History of England,* New York: Harcourt Brace & Co., 1942, pp. 124-127.

12. Ibid., pp. 369-370.

13. Ibid., p. 373.

14. Ibid., pp. 449-450.

15. Ibid., p. 450.

16. Ibid., p. 450.

17. Ibid., p. 451.

18. John Locke, *Two Treatises of Government: A Critical Edition,* ed., by Peter Lasleth, Cambridge University Press, 1960.

19. Peter Laslett, "The English Revolution and Locke's Two Treatises of Government," *Cambridge Historical Journal,* Vol. 12.

20. John Stuart Mill, "On Liberty," *Utilitarianism, On Liberty, Essay on Bentham,* Mary Warnock, ed., New York: Meridan Books, 1962, pp. 125-250.

21. Adam Smith, *An Inquiry into the Nature and Causes of the Wealth of Nations,* Edwin Cannan, ed., London University Paperpacks, 1950.

22. *The Encylopedia of Philosophy,* Vol. 4, Paul Edwards, ed., New York: Macmillan Publishing Col, Inc. & The Free Press, 1967, p. 458.

23. Robert Paul Wolff, *The Poverty of Liberalism,* Boston: Beacon Press, 1968.

24. John Stuart Mill, op. cit., p. 135.

25. Robert Dahl, *After the Revolution,* New Haven & London: Yale University Press, 1971, pp. 119-121.

26. This point is developed in the third chapter of *On Liberty.*

27. Stokeley Carmichael & Charles V. Hamilton, *Black Power: The Politics of Liberation in America,* New York: Vintage Books, 1967.

28. I do not mean that all who sought black and women's liberation are liberals. It is the case that black liberation was first pursued by liberals. I am not sure that the same can be said for the women's movement.

29. "There are again two methods of removing the causes of faction: the one by destroying the liberty which is essential to its existence; the other, by giving to every citizen the same opinions, the same passions, and the same interests. It could never be more truly said than of the first remedy, that it is worse than the disease. Liberty is to faction, what air is to fire, an ailment without which it instantly expires. But it could not be a less folly to abolish liberty, which is essential to political life, because it nourishes faction, than it would be to wish the annihilation of air, which is essential to animal life, because it imparts fire to its destructive agency.

"The second expedient is as impracticable, as the first would be unwise. As long as the reason of man continues fallible, and he is at liberty to exercise it, different opinions will be formed. As long as the connection subsists between his reason and his self-love, his opinions and his passions will have a reciprocal influence on each other; and the former will be objects to which the latter will attach themselves. The diversity in the faculties of men from which the rights of property originate, is not less an unseparable obstacle to a uniformity of interests.

"The latent causes of faction are thus sown in the nature of man, and we see them every where brought into different degrees of activity." (James Madison, "The Federalist No. 10," *The Federalist,* Jacob E, Cooke, ed., Connecticut: Wesleyan University Press, 1961, p. 58.
   30. Abrams v. U.S., 250 U.S., 616, 624.

Notes to Chapter 5

   1. Initially, the Industrial Revolution was said to begin in the eighteenth century. Subsequently, some historians maintain that its roots can be found in England much earlier. This claim need not concern us. Even if it were true, it would prove that social conditions and psychological attitudes were *ready* for industrialization. It would also show that an embryonic industrialization had begun. Those who invented liberalism were members of the status quo system.
   2. Liberty is not desired as a *sole* end. There are two ways in which liberty can be treated in liberal theory. It can be valued only as a necessary means to intellectual and emotional development. This is the view of philosophers like John Locke. It can be prized for its instrumental value *and* its intrinsic value. John Stuart Mill's *On Liberty* and James Madison's tenth *Federalist* paper interpret liberty in both ways.
   One of the best discussions of the role of liberty in society can be found in John Dewey's *Freedom and Culture.* (New York: Capricorn Books, 3rd edition, 1963.)
   3. The materialism endorsed in this section is a minimal one. Material needs must be satisfied, but other things may, as well. Spiritualism and mentalism are ruled out only as replacements for material satisfaction. They may *supervene* material development.

Notes to Chapter 6

   1. Supporting evidence is cited in note 2 of Chapter 3
   2. Edward Walter, "Individual Rights in a Limited Environment," *Philosophy for a Humanistic Society,* Alfred E. Koenig, ed., University Press, 1980.
   3. Recent statistics show that the chronically poor have fared worse than any other group in the recession of 1980. Blacks and other minorities have higher rates of unemployment. This is not surprising because these people do not usually have strong factions (unions) fighting for their interests. They occupy socially and economically inferior positions because they are mostly semiskilled or unskilled workers.
   4. In 1980, the American economy was in a precarious state. As has been indicated, the unhappy economic condition was brought about partially by timid governmental policies which were adopted because the leaders of the Carter administration believed that resources are running out. There may be no quick revival of the economy because once a negative attitude toward the economy sets in, it remains for quite a while. The downcast economic attitude that characterized American business activity in the 1930s was unshakable until the beginning of World War II.

The economists who supported the Carter administration's policies do not take into account the fact that once a "recession-attitude" is produced, it is not controllable. The Carter administration desired a small recession in order to reduce inflation, but when the recession came it was more persistent than anticipated. The moral is that you cannot instill a negative attitude in people and, then, dispel it overnight.

The point is that, just as the American economy could have been revived by 1936 if the will of the people were up to it, the American economy can revive in several years if the right policies are adopted and the people are ready for them.

5. John Dewey, *The Quest for Certainty*, New York: Capricorn Books, Third Edition, 1960, Chapter X.

6. The expressions "moral objectivism" and "moral subjectivism" are chosen because they are the best available. Moral philosophers have not agreed on general moral categories. I choose these expressions because objectivism implies that morality relies on actual conditions and subjectivism relies on "states of mind." In some sense, utilitarian, deontological, and theistic moral theories determine moral status by reference to actual conditions. Conversely, subjectivism, emotivism, and ethical relativity make subjective states the basis of morality.

Despite the general adequacy of these two moral categories, their designations are misleading. Utilitarianism refers to subjective states, and some versions of ethical relativity hold that moral rules are limitedly objective. Nevertheless, there are no better general category terms available.

7. Karl Marx, "The German Ideology, Part I," *The Marx-Engels Reader*, Robert C. Tucker, ed., New York: W. W. Norton & Co., Inc., 1972, pp. 186-188.

8. Sidney Hook observed that people are motivated by more than economic interests. For example, if economic factors determined social choices, the working classes in all countries would have opposed the First World War. They did not follow their economic interests, as many people and factions have not in numerous cases. Sidney Hook, *Marx and the Marxists*, New York: D. Van Nostrand Company, Inc., 1955, p. 39.

9. When communists fight among themselves, they accuse each other of being covert bourgeois. The frequency with which this charge is made and the diversity of situations to which it is applied lead a neutral observer to conclude that it is used to cover more ordinary motivations, such as the desire to achieve political power for ego gratification.

10. Brian Crozier, *The Future of Communist Power*, London: Eyre & Spottiswoode, 1970, p. 180.

Notes to Chapter 7

1. Daniel P. Harrison, *Social Forecasting Methodology: Suggestions for Research*, New York: Russell Sage Foundation, 1976, p. 4.

2. Jay Forrester, *World Dynamics*, Cambridge, MA: Wright-Allen Press, 1971.

3. Mihajlo Mesarovich and Eduard Pestel, *Mankind at the Turning Point*, New York: E. P. Dutton and Co., 1974.

4. Harrison, op. cit., p. 24.

5. Ibid., p. 20.

6. Kenneth E. Boulding, *Economics As A Science*, New York: McGraw-Hill Book Company, 1970, pp. 113-114.

7. H. W. Arndt, *Economic Lessons of the Nineteen Thirties*, New York: Augustus M. Kelley, 3rd Edition, 1965, p. 15.

8. Ibid., p. 16.

9. Herbert Hoover, "Economic Individualism," *Crisis of the American Dream*, John Tipple, ed., New York: Pegasus, 1968, pp. 189-190.

10. Douglas F. Dowd, *The Twisted Dream: Capitalist Development in the United States Since 1776*, Cambridge, MA: Winthrop Publishers, Inc., 1974, p. 96.

11. Arndt, op. cit., pp. 16-18.

12. F. C. Walcott, "How Much Can Government Help?", *Proceedings of the Academy of Political Science*, edited by P. T. Moon, Columbus University, 1932, p. 121.

13. Alan Bullock, *Hitler, A Study in Tyranny*, Revised Edition, New York: Harper Torchbooks, 1964, pp. 356-358.

14. J. M. Keynes, *Essays in Persuasion*, New York: The Norton Library, 1963, pp. 365-366.

15. D. W. Fryer, *World Economic Development*, New York: McGraw-Hill Book Company, 1965, p. 600.

16. *The Outlook for Economic Growth, 1960-1980*, The Organization for Economic Co-operation and Development, May 1970.

17. William L. Oltmans, ed., *On Growth: The Crisis of Exploding Population and Resource Depletion*, New York: Capricorn Books, 1974, p. 416.

18. Ibid., p. 49.

19. S. Fred Singer, "Limits to Arab Oil Power," *Foreign Policy*, Number 30 (Spring 1978), pp. 36-37.

20. Robert S. Pindyck, "OPEC's Threat to the West," *Foreign Policy*, Number 30 (Spring 1978), pp. 36-37.

21. M. A. Adelman, "Need for Caution Over Prices," a paper read at the Workshop on Supply-Demand Analysis at Brookhaven National Laboratory, Upton, New York, 6/1/1977.

Notes to Chapter 8

1. Robert H. Williams, "Fossil Fuel Resources," Barry Commoner, Howard Boksenbaum, Michael Corr (ed.), *Energy and Human Welfare—A Critical Analysis, Volume II: Alternative Technologies for Power Production*, New York: Macmillan Publishing Co., Inc., 1975, pp. 9-10.

2. Recent research indicates, for example, that there is more recoverable oil in the United States than was imagined only a few years ago.

3. Williams, op. cit., p. 2.

4. T. A. Hendricks, "Resources of Oil, Gas, and Natural Gas Liquids in the U.S. and the World," *U.S. Geological Survey Circular 523* (1965).

M. K. Hubert, "Energy Resources," Freeman (ed.), *Resources and Man,* Committee on Resources and Man, National Academy of Sciences, National Research Council, 1969.

5. Potential Gas Committee, *Potential Supply of Natural Gas in the U.S. as of Dec. 31, 1970* (1971).

6. Paul Averitt, "Coal Resources of the United States, January 1, 1967," *U.S. Geological Survey Bulletin 1275* (1969).

7. Herman Kahn, William Brown, and Leon Martel, *The Next 200 Years,* New York: William Morrow and Company, Inc., 1976, p. 63.

8. Arthur M. Squires, "The Fossil Fuel Development Gap," Commoner, Boksenbaum, Corr, op. cit., p. 44.

9. Robert Pindyck, "The American Energy Debate," a working paper written at M.I.T., January 1980, to appear in *The Public Interest.*

10. Michael Fortune, "Synthetic Fuels from Coal," Commoner, Boksenbaum, Corr, op. cit., p. 79.

11. Ibid., p. 81.

12. Ibid., p. 98.

13. Terri Aaronson, "The Black Box: The Fuel Cell," Commoner, Boksenbaum, Corr, op. cit., pp. 102-116.

14. Ibid., pp. 102-103.

15. Richard C. Bailie, "Wasted Solids as an Energy Resource," Commoner, Boksenbaum, Corr, op. cit., pp. 117-130.

16. Ibid., p. 126.

17. Ibid., pp. 127-129.

18. Paul L. Joskow and Robert S. Pindyck, "Synthetic Fuels," *A E I Journal on Government and Society,* September/October 1979, p. 43.

19. Harry K. Girvetz, *The Evolution of Liberalism,* London: Collier-Macmillan Ltd., 1963, pp. 206-209.

20. Robert H. Williams, "Fission Fuel Resources," Commoner, Boksenbaum, Corr, op. cit., pp. 24-42.

21. Ibid., p. 27.

22. Ibid., p. 29.

23. Ibid., p. 38.

24. Ibid., p. 40.

25. David J. Rose, "Controlled Nuclear Fusion: Status and Outlook," Commoner, Boksenbaum, Corr, op. cit., pp. 148-153.

26. K. S. Shrader-Frechette, *Nuclear Power and Public Policy,* London: D. Reidel Publishing Company, 1980, p. 7.

27. Ibid., pp. 30-35.

28. Ibid., p. 14.

29. Marc Kramer, David Fenner, Joseph Klarmann, and Robert H. Williams, "Geothermal Energy," Commoner, Boksenbaum, Corr, op. cit., pp. 161-186.

30. Ibid., p. 172.

31. Ibid., pp. 163-165.

32. Ibid., p. 165.
33. Ibid., p. 170.
34. Ibid., p. 182.
35. Arthur R. Tamplin, "Solar Energy," Commoner, Boksenbaum, Corr, op. cit., pp. 187-188.
36. Ibid., p. 188.
37. Ibid., pp. 188-191.
38. Ibid., pp. 191-192.
39. Ibid., p. 192.
40. Ibid., p. 199.
41. Ibid., p. 200.
42. Ibid., p. 201.

Notes to Chapter 9

1. F. E. Banks, "Problems of Mineral Supply," *Future Resources and World Development*, Paul Rogers, ed., New York and London: Plenum Press, 1976.
2. Herman Kahn, William Brown, and Leon Martel, *The Next 200 Years*, New York: William Morrow and Company, Inc., 1976, pp. 85-87.
3. Dennis L. Meadows, *et al.*, *Dynamics of Growth in a Future World*, Cambridge, MA: Wright-Allen Press, 1974, pp. 372-373.
4. Kahn, op. cit., p. 90.
5. Peter T. Flawn, *Mineral Resources*, Chicago, New York, San Francisco: Rand McNally & Company, 1966, pp. 293-294.
6. Kahn, op. cit., p. 91.
7. Ibid., p. 92.
8. Commission on Critical Choices for Americans, *Vital Resources*, Volume 1, Lexington, MA: Lexington Books, 1977, p. 133.
9. Ibid., p. 133.
10. Ibid., p. 131.
11. Ibid., p. 139.
12. *Raw Materials and Foreign Policy*, International Economic Studies Institute, Washington, D.C., 1976, p. 7.
13. Ibid., p. 8.
14. *Vital Resources*, op. cit., p. 143.
15. Ibid., p. 144.
16. *Raw Materials and Foreign Policy*, op. cit., p. 66.
17. Ibid., p. 67.
18. Ibid., p. 68.
19. *Vital Resources*, op. cit., p. 135.
20. Ibid., p. 130.
21. Ibid., pp. 148-149.
22. Ibid., p. 131.

Notes to Chapter 10

1. Meadows, Randers, *et al.*, *The Limits of Growth*, New York: Signet Books, New American Library Association, 1963, p. 4.
2. Ibid., pp. 176-179.
3. Marston Bates, *Expanding Population in a Shrinking World*, New York: American Library Association, 1963, p. 4.
4. Ibid., p. 4.
5. *World Population Growth and Responses*, Washington, D.C.: Population Reference Bureau, 1976, p. 269.
6. Ibid., p. 269.
7. Ibid., p. 267.
8. Ibid., p. 266.
9. Bates, op. cit., p. 4.
10. Ibid., p. 4.
11. W. D. Borrie, *Population, Environment, and Society*, New Zealand: Aukland University Press/Oxford University Press, 1972, p. 19.
12. Ibid., p. 19.
13. Ibid., p. 21.
14. Ibid., p. 23.
15. Ibid., p. 57.
16. *World Population Growth and Responses*, op. cit., p. 7.
17. Borrie, op. cit., p. 24.
18. *World Population Growth and Responses*, op. cit., p. 19.
19. Borrie, op. cit., p. 30.
20. *World Population Growth and Responses*, op. cit., p. 3.
21. Ibid., p. 4.
22. Borrie, op. cit., pp. 52-53.
23. Ibid., p. 45.
24. Ibid., p. 47.
25. Ibid., p. 49.
26. *World Population Growth and Responses*, op. cit., p. 180.
27. Borrie, op. cit., p. 57.
28. Ibid., p. 67.
29. *World Population Growth and Responses*, op. cit., p. 78.
30. Ibid., p. 2.
31. Ibid., p. 265.
32. Ibid., p. 265.
33. Ibid., pp. 19-20.
34. Ibid., p. 20.
35. Borrie, op. cit., pp. 67-68.
36. Ibid., p. 68.
37. *World POpulation Growth and Responses*, op. cit., p. 78.
38. Herman Kahn, *The Next 200 Years*, New York: William Morrow and Company, Inc., 1976, p. 136.

39. *The CBS Almanac 1977*, Maplewood, N.J.: Hammond Almanac, Inc., p. 545.
40. *World Population Growth and Responses*, op. cit., pp. 8-9.
41. Ibid., p. 11.
42. Ibid., p. 14.
43. Ibid., p. 14.
44. Borrie, op. cit., pp. 72-73.

Notes to Chapter 11

1. Study of Critical Environmental Problems, *Man's Impact on the Global Environment: Assessments and Recommendations for Action*, MA: MIT Press, 1971.
2. P. J. W. Saunders, *The Estimation of Pollution Damage*, Manchester: Manchester University Press, 1976, p. 32.
3. Ibid., p. 31.
4. Ibid., p. 11.
5. Ibid., p. 15.
6. Ibid., pp. 34-35.
7. Ibid., p. 35.
8. Ibid., p. 35.
9. R. Scott Russell, "Contamination of the Biosphere with Radioactivity," *Environmental Management: Science and Politics*, Morton and Marsha Gordon (eds.), Boston: Allyn and Bacon, Inc., 1972, p. 69.
10. Saunders, op. cit., p. 37.
11. Ibid., p. 38.
12. Ibid., pp. 39-40.
13. Ibid., p. 41.
14. Ibid., p. 23.
15. Ibid., p. 43.
16. Ibid., p. 43.
17. Ibid., p. 45.
18. Ibid., p. 47.
19. Ibid., p. 109.

Index